May Babies

Real Mom's Real Birth Stories

May Babies

Real Mom's Real Birth Stories

Foreword

This book is a compilation of birth stories, from twenty-three women, who met in a social media group for expecting mothers due in May of 2016.

This book is dedicated to all the women of
"Babies Due May 2016"

I have met so many beautiful and kind women from this group, each one with a different background and from all walks of life.
Most of us joined this group when we first became pregnant in the summer of 2015,
I was pregnant with my 5th child when I joined.
This was the first time I had discovered that groups like this were a thing.
These amazing, strong women of "Babies Due May 2016" have become like sisters, in the sense that I can still share anything with them and know that we are always here to support each other, just as we were when we started this journey together.

Thank you!

With Special Thanks

to

Dana Schnyder

For the
Beautiful Cover Art

Preface

Members and Due Dates

APRIL 11TH
- Amal Burkett - TEAM PINK

APRIL 23RD
- Karabeth Davis - TEAM BLUE - Jayden Thomas Pedigo

APRIL 28TH
- Tika Gitzen - TEAM BLUE - Gannon David Gitzen

MAY 4TH
- Jeanette Tharp - TEAM PINK

- Misty Shettles - TEAM BLUE - Collin James

MAY 19TH
- Brandi Long Walter - TEAM BLUE - Ezekiel Jerald

MAY 20TH
- Bethany Adkins - TEAM PINK - Suzanne-Elizabeth

MAY 27TH
- Ashley Franklin - TEAM PINK

MAY 28TH
- Danielle Bair - TEAM BLUE - Cooper James Bair

- Amanda Collins - TEAM BLUE - Declan Garrett Collins

JUNE 2ND
- Maranda Joy Snyder - TEAM PINK

JUNE 6TH
- Ashley Smith - TEAM BLUE - Macsen Paul Stone

JUNE 12TH
- Dana Schnyder - TEAM BLUE

MAY 8TH

- Shayla Kieneker - TEAM BLUE

- Thorn Tillson Epp - TEAM PINK

MAY 10TH

- Katie Theuer- TEAM PINK

MAY 12TH

- Linsy Porelle - TEAM BLUE

MAY 13TH

- Tasha Crabb - TEAM PINK - Karleigh Mae

- Alicia Ward - TEAM BLUE

MAY 14TH

- Casey Lowe - TEAM PINK

MAY 16TH

- Jessica Pataky - TEAM PINK

- Shamala Bunch-Sparks - TEAM PINK - Makenzi Lynn sparks

MAY 18TH

- Bailey Nicole Kemper - TEAM PINK

Chapters

Each story is written by the mothers, with light editing.

Lucky

Amal Burkett

I was 36 weeks on March 16, 2016, when at 9:20 a.m., while lying in my bed sleeping, all of a sudden, I woke up thinking I had peed myself. I called my mom and told her what had happened; she told me to get up and walk around to see if I was leaking water. When I got out of bed and bent over, sure enough, a gush came out! My water had indeed, broken!!! So, I called my mom back and told her it was definitely my water that had broken. My mom came over to my house and drove me to the hospital, where I was admitted into Labor and Delivery. I began preparing for the birth of my daughter. After being in the hospital for 24 hours in labor, the doctor came to check my cervix for progress. That's when they discovered that my water had not entirely broken.

Up until that point, I had been in hard labor for 10 hours, having back to back contractions. Finally, the doctor popped my water the rest of the way. After that, it only took about 2 hours before I felt the urge to use the restroom. The nurse informed me that it was time to push, but I decided to go ahead and wait another 30 minutes before I would begin pushing. Once I started pushing, it would only be about 30 minutes before Hayden entered the world. I remember when she came out, I kept asking the doctor why isn't she crying. I had this preconceived notion from watching television and movies that my baby would come into the world immediately, screaming and crying. So when she didn't, I had a brief moment of fear. Little did I know, this would be the least of my concerns. It wasn't until months later that we would find out that my baby had a brain tumor. They had to suction the fluid from her nose and mouth to clear her throat, only then did she begin to cry. I was immediately in tears. They laid her on my chest, and at that moment, I realized what true love was. This was the second most joyous moment of my life! The first being, Hayden surviving the brain tumor.

I didn't want to let her go, and I didn't want to have her go to the nursery. I wanted to hold my precious baby in my arms for the rest of my life. Nothing is more significant than motherhood! During my whole pregnancy, I was terrified I would be a horrible mother. I never wanted kids, but when the doctor sat that tiny 5 pound 11-ounce baby on my chest, my whole world changed. She was born at 6:23 pm. She was and is my soulmate! My daughter has made me a better, stronger woman and continues to show me what true love is every day.

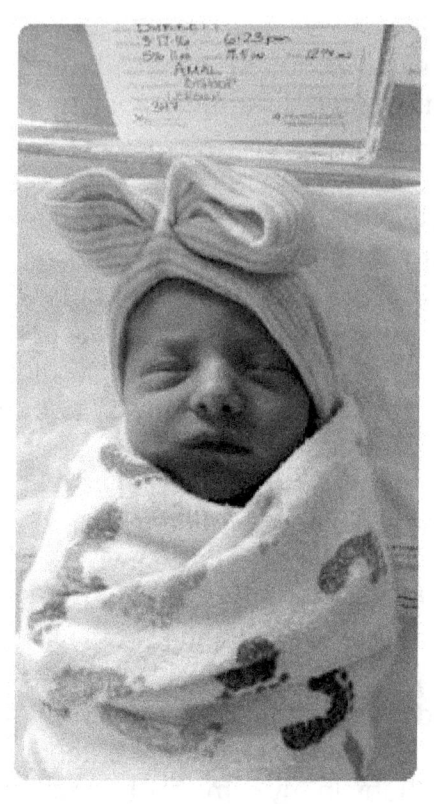

Hayden
Date of Birth: March 17th, 2016
Birth Time: 6:23 pm.
Weight: 5 pounds 11 ounces
Height: 19½ inches long

Amal Burkett

Bailey Nicole Kemper

March 17, 2016

"Please pray/ keep one of our members in your thoughts! My bestie Amal has been in labor since 9:30 am yesterday at 36 weeks!"

"Ependymomas, also known as "WHO Grade 2" is the third most common type of brain tumor in children, following Astrocytoma and Medulloblastoma, all are relatively rare, with approximately 200 cases being diagnosed in the US each year, in children and adults, under the age of twenty-five. The average age of diagnosis is between four and six years old. The underlying cause and basic biology of the tumors are not fully understood."

For more information on "WHO Grade 2", please check out the websites provided below.

https://www.stjude.org/disease/ependymoma.html

https://www.cancer.net/cancer-types/ependymoma-childhood/stages-and-grades

Conceived on the Pill

Karabeth Davis

Jayden Thomas Pedigo graced my life on April 6th, 2016.

Now, I feel it's essential to my story that I share a little bit about the pregnancy. Jayden is the youngest of four children. His father Jesse and I each have a child from a previous relationship. They were both 9-years-old at the time, and we already had a 19-month-old together. We were done having kids! I was on birth control, but we ended up pregnant anyway. I did not want to be pregnant at all! So, I scheduled an appointment for an abortion. The day before my scheduled abortion, I received a call from the clinic telling me that my insurance had lapsed, and they would be canceling my appointment! I was devastated, and I didn't want another baby! We began to do everything we could to gather money to have an abortion. It took us one week to collect the money, but I had changed my mind; I didn't want to go through with it anymore. I had already had two previous abortions, one before Jesse and one with him (before Jaxson, my only planned pregnancy). I cried a lot, and I hated everything! I didn't want this baby, but I didn't want another abortion. I was afraid for my mental health with the result of either decision I made. After that, my pregnancy was fairly textbook. Except for me being miserable carrying a baby that I didn't really want at the time, everything went great! I went to a scheduled doctor's appointment on April 4th. My doctor did a membrane sweep and said to me,

"See you in the next 24 hours".

She was only off by a little bit too. On April 5th, contractions started, so I called my doctor. She tells me to wait before coming in. A few hours later, I'm like fuck this! I go to the hospital and check into Labor & Delivery, where they confirm, I was having mild contractions. They told me to go home and wait it out there. Okay, cool! I'm down with spending as little time as possible in the hospital. I woke up the next morning around eight, dying in pain! I was either dying, or this was labor! I called my doctor around 11 am and went to her office at 12:30 pm. After making it to her office, she checked me and said,

"Get to the hospital! It's baby time! I'll be right behind you."

She was! She was less than 10 minutes behind us. I made it to the hospital at around 1:30 pm. I opted for an epidural, but the epidural didn't seem to work. The nurse went to call the anesthesiologist while my doctor checked my cervix for progression.

My doctor tells me, *"Try to push,"* and then says,

"Okay, stop! I'm going to get things ready. Call whoever should be here."

So, Jesse called my mom, who lives 5 minutes away from the hospital and two minutes later my doctor comes back and says,

"Try to push again."

Followed by...

"Really push! One more!"

BAM!!! Just like that, I had a baby! My mind and body were prepared to push for a long time. He was on my chest, and I still had no idea what was going on! In less than five minutes, I had had a baby. I had barely wrapped my head around the fact that I was pushing, and now I had a baby. The way that baby spoke to my soul the second he hit my skin, is something I could never describe in words to anyone. I may not have wanted this baby, but man, did I need him. Sometimes the things we don't really want are precisely the things that we need. Even now, when I think back on this day, it all seemed to happen in such a Blur. This kid still speaks to my soul on an extraordinary level.

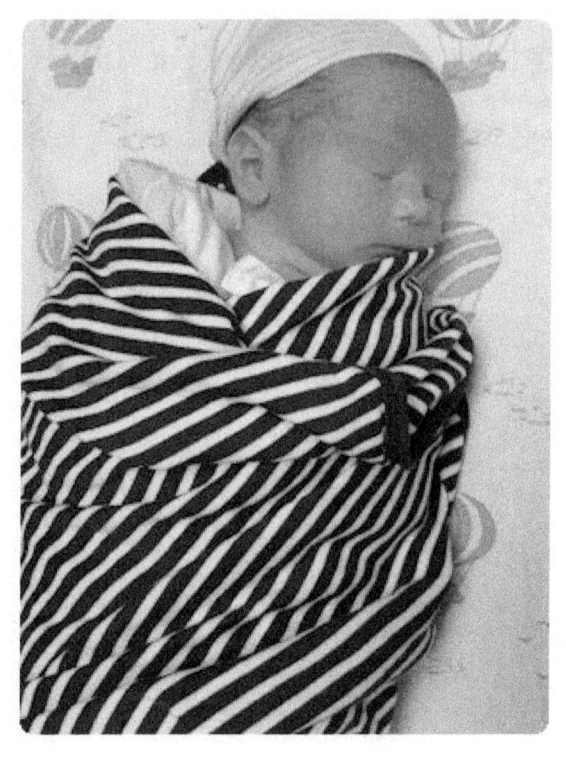

Jayden Thomas Pedigo
Date of Birth: April 6th, 2016
Birth Time: 3:35 pm
Weight: 6 pounds 6 ounces
Height: 18¼ inches long

Karabeth Davis

Wet Feet

Tika Gitzen

My labor was induced due to gestational diabetes and reduced movement from the baby. I had been in active labor for three days before receiving a C-section. I chose to get the epidural; it took over an hour to get in, and we needed the top anesthesiologist on staff to come in to do the spinal. During that time, my water broke all over my husband's feet. My husband had been standing in front of me, so I could hold onto him while they gave me the epidural. I thought it was hilarious because the doctor had already broken my water, but it had only been trickling; this covered the whole floor. The staff let me labor for 8 hours before they told me they were going to need to do a c-section. Gannon's head was stuck, and he was getting stressed. I was induced on Thursday, April 21st. On Saturday, April 23rd, at 11:29 pm, the most beautiful little human I've ever seen, came into the world with a beautiful, healthy cry. My husband went with the baby to do the measurements and check for all fingers and toes, etc., while the doctor sewed me back up. I then went to a recovery room to be with my baby and breastfeed. The staff would continue to make sure everything was ok with us. After a while in the recovery room, we went to a regular baby room, and I was there for two days before being released.

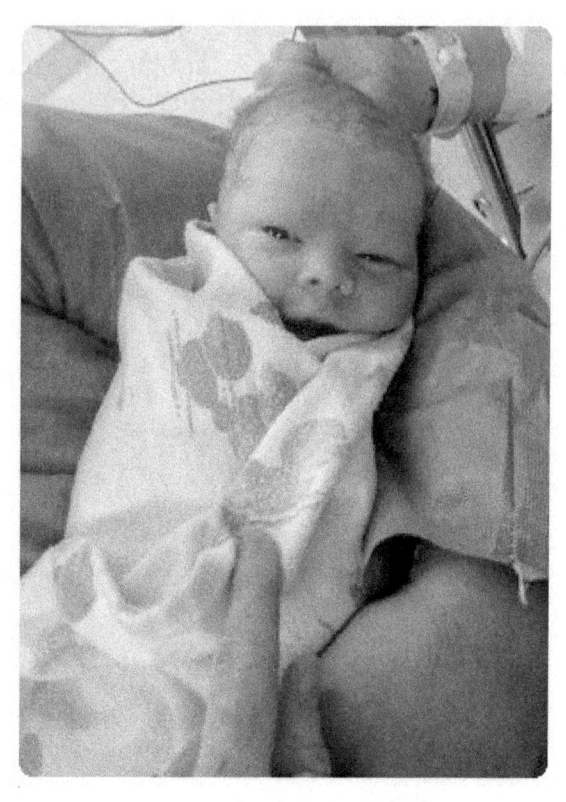

Gannon David Gitzen
Birth Time: 11:29 pm
Birth Date: April 23rd, 2016
Weighing 7 pounds 1 ounce
Height: 20½ inches long

Tika Gitze

Tika Gitzen

April 24, 2016

"Here he is! Gannon David Gitzen, 7lbs 1oz 20 1/2 inches, born at 11:29 pm on April 23rd. Delivered via c-section because I stopped dilating at 7cm. He's so perfect, I'm so in love!"

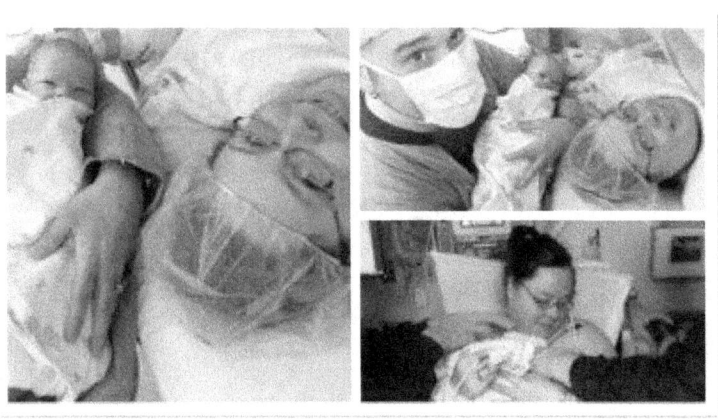

Birth Tail

Shamala Bunch-Sparks

I went to the hospital at 11:45 pm on April 25th, 2016, so I could start my induction at midnight. I was being induced at 37+1 due to gestational hypertension. I was hooked up to the monitors, and luckily I was dilated. My cervix had thinned out just enough that I didn't need any other form of induction except for Pitocin. My blood pressure was high, so they talked about doing a c-section if it didn't lower on its own. Thankfully, after settling in and being hooked up to the monitors, my blood pressure began to drop. My husband was able to sleep on and off the entire night. When I started feeling the pain, I requested to have the epidural. After multiple failed attempts at the epidural, I was told they would try one last time. On that last attempt, they were able to get the epidural in.

At last, I was finally able to get some rest. It was 7 am, and the nurses were working on shift changes. The nurses didn't bother to come into the room. I wasn't rechecked for progression until after they were done, even though I was feeling pressure and calling for the nurse. When I was checked again, the nurse told me…

"It's baby time!"

She opened the door, yelling out that she needed the doctor. When the doctor came into the room, I could see he was still tired from having just woke up. He continued to get ready to deliver the baby. It was less than twenty minutes after the doctor came in before I had Makenzi. She arrived at 7:20 am, weighing 6 pounds 7 ounces. To our surprise, she was born with "a tail." After delivery, I continued bleeding heavily! They poked me in the upper leg to clot my blood. After this, I vowed I wouldn't get another epidural if I were to get pregnant again. I ended up walking away with severe bruising on my lower back from several failed attempts. We didn't find until August 19th of that same year that the tail had no consistency, and it was a mass of fat tethered to her spine. She indeed had spina bifida, that had never come up on the ultrasounds. It wouldn't have made a difference anyway, I loved her from the start.

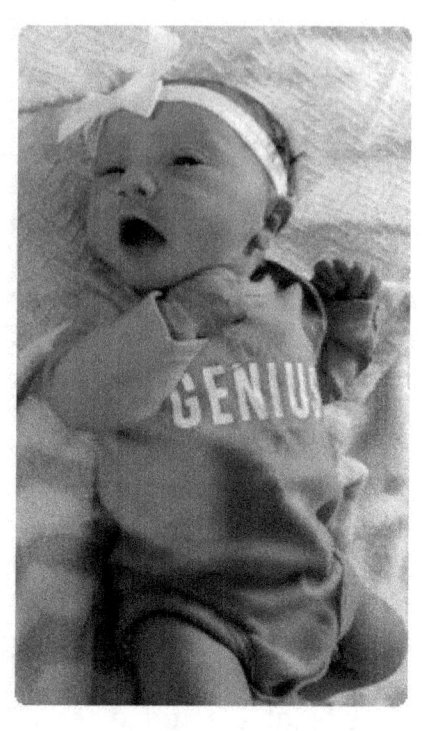

Makenzi Sparks
Birth Date: April 26th, 2016
Birth Time: 7:20 am
Weight:
Height:

Shamala Bunch-Sparks

Shamala Bunch-Sparks

April 26, 2016

"Born 7:20 this morning 6pounds 7oz
Ms. Makenzi Lynn Sparks

She has a "Tail" they think is a relation to Spina Bifida so
they will be sending a neurosurgeon in to look at her,
X-Ray it and possible surgery."

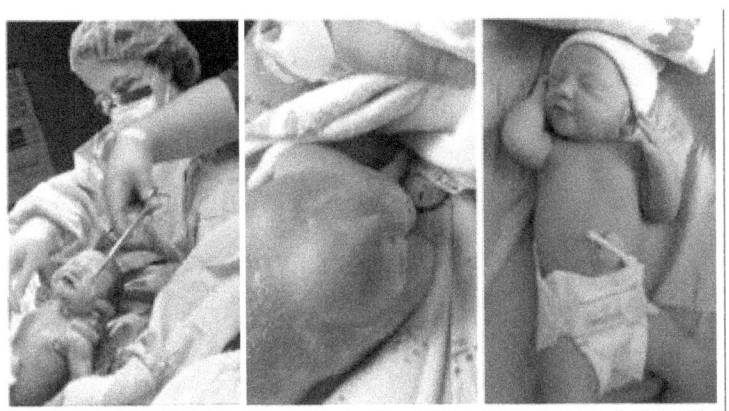

"The word Spina Bifida means "split spine" in Latin. Spina bifida is a congenital disability "birth defect." It is a rare condition around the world with fewer than 200,000 people with the defect, but in the United States, it is more common. Around 1,500 to 2,000 babies are born each year with spina bifida. There are three types of Spina Bifida. "Spina Bifida Occulta, Meningocele, and Myelomeningocele," each very different in their degree of severity, but thanks to the advances in modern medicine, 90% of babies born today with this defect go on to live to be adults, and most will lead full lives."

For more information on Spina Bifida, please check out the websites provided below.

www.spinabifidaassociation.org

www.webmd.com/parenting/baby/spina-bifida

Liberty

Jeanette Tharp

April 18th,
I went to the Doctor today in the hopes of
scheduling a planned c-section. From the
beginning of my pregnancy, the Doctor would tell
me that a VBAC was not an option.

April 20th,
Last night I went to L&D with a fever of 101. I was
pretty adamant about not getting the IV in my hand;
it just freaks me out so bad. The nurse I have
doesn't want to put the IV in the bend of my elbow,
so she compromises with the side of my right arm
only to blew the vein on it. I start freaking out a bit
because I've never seen that happen before. The
head nurse in charge comes in, and she tries the
left inside of my elbow. She couldn't draw blood but
continue to put the IV in anyways, causing a huge
and painful lump of fluid to form. While I was crying
from the pain, I have nurses telling me to stop
crying because it doesn't hurt. My husband pulls
the sleeve of the hospital gown up and says,

"What the Fuck! Why is it doing that?" and then the nurse says,

"Oh, I guess it did hurt, huh?"

How am I supposed to trust this hospital and its staff to give a spinal and deliver my baby safely when the nurses can't even put an IV in my arm. I'm terrified to get the spinal/epidural for c-section, but what other options do I have?! Half of me is like nope I can stay home and have this baby in the bathtub, not being forced to on my back, no charting every feed, diaper, etc. just comfy in my bed.

I know it will be an anesthesiologist who performs the spinal. Still, the lack of respect from doctors and nurses makes me leary. During the whole ordeal, one of the nurses lost the veil blood they had drawn, and I never ended up receiving the IV fluid.

April 24th,
I'm becoming increasingly frustrated with the lack of control I had when it came to labor and delivery. I already have no say in the date of my c-section, and now I am being told I have no say in the type of

anesthesia. I want general anesthesia, not local, but doctor doom says there's No chance in hell. Delayed cord clamping, not a chance, skin to skin who knows, and vaccinations are mandated in the state of California. I feel helpless! Maybe it's an inconvenience since the hospital is going through a massive remodel in the L&D ward, but this is devastating.

April 26th,
Tomorrow is my scheduled c-section, so I thought I would ask my Doctor a few questions.

Me:
"What kind of sutures are you planning on using?"

Doctor:
"Whatever kind I feel like."

Me:
"Who do I talk to about the possibility of getting general anesthesia vs. local?"

Doctor:
"Nobody because there's not a chance in hell of that happening. Why don't you let me be the

Doctor!"
Me:
(Starts crying)

Doctor:
"Any more questions? No...."

This birth is already the most traumatizing thing to ever happen to me, and it hasn't even happened yet. My c-section is tomorrow, it's too late to find a new doctor at this point, and I have a level of anxiety that is outrageous. I'm terrified to death of my Doctor. I'm frightened of being paralyzed. My heart rate has skyrocketed to 160 when they put the IV in, and I'm afraid of passing out during the spinal. My Doctor has literally made me cry at every single appointment I had with him. I've avoided talking and going to him as much a possible and my husband doesn't understand why I think he hates me.

April 27th,
Liberty is here! 7 pounds 1 ounce and nursing like a champ!

April 28th,

"Traumatic" doesn't begin to describe yesterday! I ended up getting put under after the Doctor and anesthesiologist "ripped me apart" and then I was verbally assaulted by an asshole because I had a panic attack before the spinal! The anesthesiologist was pissed! My doctor told him to put me to sleep and then went off on me. The hospital has six of us crammed into one room right now and there are not enough rooms available "due to construction." My insurance is crap, and I just want to go home!

My Doctor doesn't "Do Birth Plans"! I wanted general anesthesia, and they refused. I did really good up until I walked into the O.R. and saw all the tools on the table. There was this shoe-horn looking thing and the staples! They didn't give me any options. I was blatantly told that I don't have any "options" with the birth. If I decide against something, it's equal to breaking hospital policy. Which means they can discharge me from their care. I was told I "wasn't really distraught," and I "was just crying and shaking to manipulate the anesthesiologist to do something stupid and unsafe." I really just want to go home.

Within 24 hours post-op, I've been forcing myself to walk, I had the catheter removed, the IV capped off, used the restroom, ate, drank, etc. I'm doing everything I can to get out of here! One of the nurses is hiding in the room I'm sharing with six people to sit and play on her phone.

April 29th,
I must admit when I first saw my c-section, I got dizzy, it hurts so badly and stings when I move. They haven't stapled my incision right at ALL. Is "Medical Rape" a thing? Because that's how I feel! I'm scared, and it hurts so badly. All I want is to go home!

At one point I'm crying about being depressed 48hrs postpartum and then right before being released from the hospital, my Dr. looks at my mom and says to her,

Doctor:
"Are you her mom? How did you manage to raise such a cry baby?"

He insulted my mother! Who does that?!

I'm absolutely horrified by my birth and the way they have left me like this. I don't want any more children solely based upon my birth experience and will be having my tubes tied!

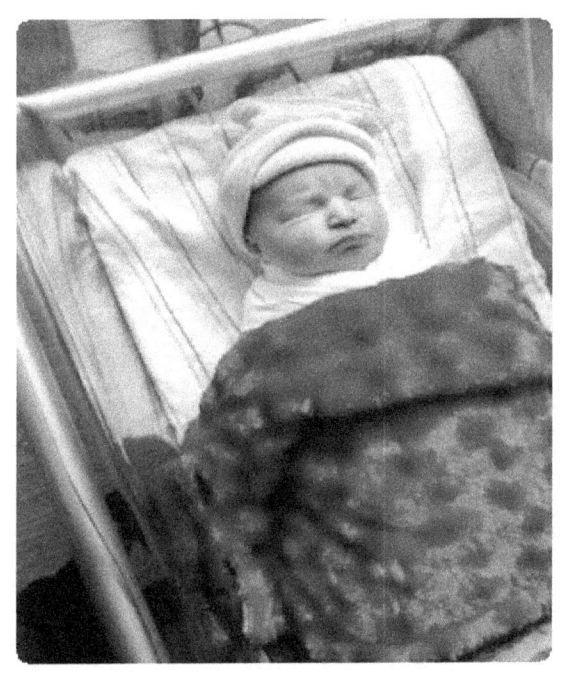

Liberty
Date of Birth: April 27th, 2016
Time: 1:01 pm
Weight: 7pounds 1ounce
Height: 18 inches long

Jeanette Tharp

Jeanette Tharp

April 27, 2016

"Liberty is here!"

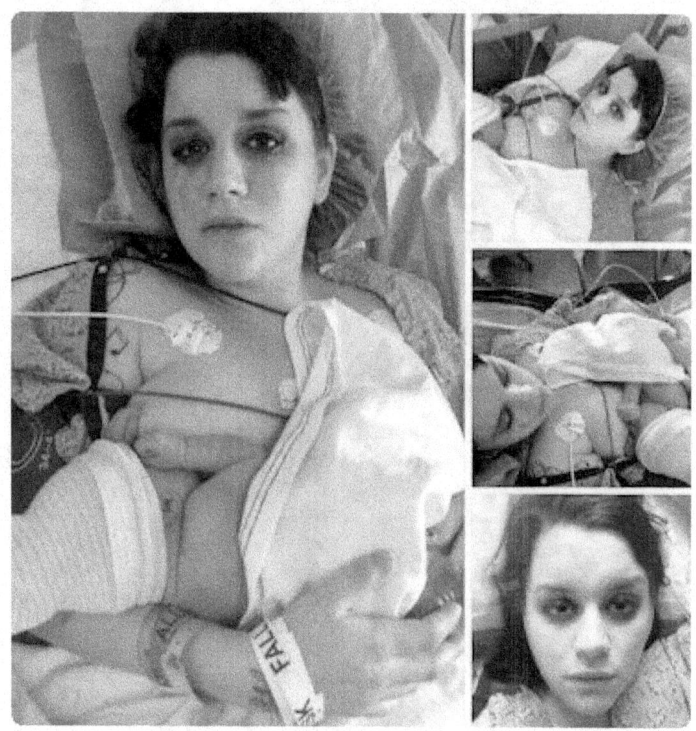

Emergency C-section

Misty Shettles

It was April 29th, when I went in for my weekly NST (Non-Stress Test) with ultrasound included. I sat in the chair in my doctor's office; my daughter's heart rate was looking great until the very end of the allotted time for an NST. My baby's heart rate started to dip and slow down tremendously. I began to get worried! I was getting ready to get my OB when he walked into the room, with a look of concern on his face. He said to me that my daughter's heart rate had him worried. I was immediately sent over to L&D for an in-depth ultrasound and to be monitored.

I started to panic and cry because I had suffered a miscarriage at full term the previous year! I "wrangled up" my other two daughters and headed upstairs to L&D, fearing the worst. When my girls and I made it upstairs, the first thing the nurses did was get me set up in the triage room. Within about ten minutes of being in the triage room, a nurse walked in and began to tell me that my doctor had a change of plans for me. I would be delivering my baby that night. OH, HOLY, HECK!!! I was not at all prepared for what was happening. I didn't have my hospital bag, car seat, anything for my two daughters, no phone charger, and on top of it all, my husband was a four-hour drive away from our hospital.

I called my husband right away to let him know what was going on with the baby. He ended up leaving work, without even telling his boss or anyone else where he was going, or what was going on! He drove straight home first, which was on the way, but still two hours away from the hospital. My husband grabbed my hospital bag and everything else we thought we would need. Then he was back on the road again. At this point, I was hooked up to monitors and waiting to be taken back for surgery. I didn't know if my husband would make it to the hospital in time for the birth. My two girls were still in the triage room with me while all of this was going on, but thankfully, I have some awesome friends who live in the area. They sat with me in the triage room as we waited for my good friends to pick them up from the hospital. Once they were picked up, I was able to rest, while I was waiting to be taken in for surgery. The nurse came into the room to take me back for my C-Section. I began to think I was going to do it alone, but my husband made it there just in time, as they were wheeling me down the hallway to the operating room. Once I was in the operating room, I was given a spinal block. The doctor and nurses quickly got to work. Twenty minutes later, I heard the most beautiful whispers ever from my husband.

"She's here, and so tiny!"

She was 5 pounds, 12 ounces. My doctor said she was going to be at least 8 pounds.

'Umm, No!'

"Big difference, Dr. Mckenna! What happened to 8 pounds?" I shouted!

Everyone in the room started to laugh. My doctor waited to cut the umbilical cord until it stopped pulsating, and then immediately had one of the nurses place my baby on my chest. She took my breath away at first sight, with how beautifully perfect she was! Dakota was born on April 29th, at 5:38 pm.

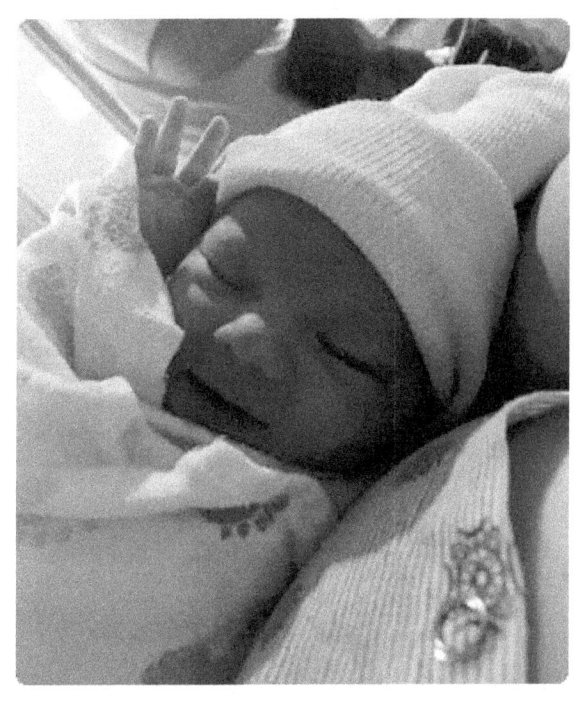

Dakota Leigh
Date of Birth: April 29th, 2016
Time: 7:32 pm
Weight: 5 pounds 12 ounces
Height: 18½ inches long

Misty Shettles

Misty Shettles

April 29, 2016

"I can't believe I'm two hours away from having my baby!"

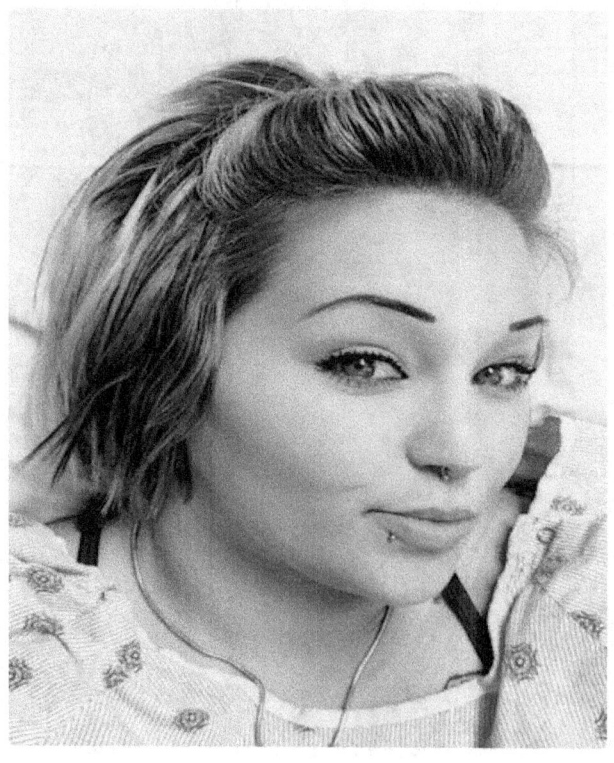

Misty Shettles

April 29, 2016

"Dakota Leigh

5.12 lbs

18.5 in long

Head full of hair"

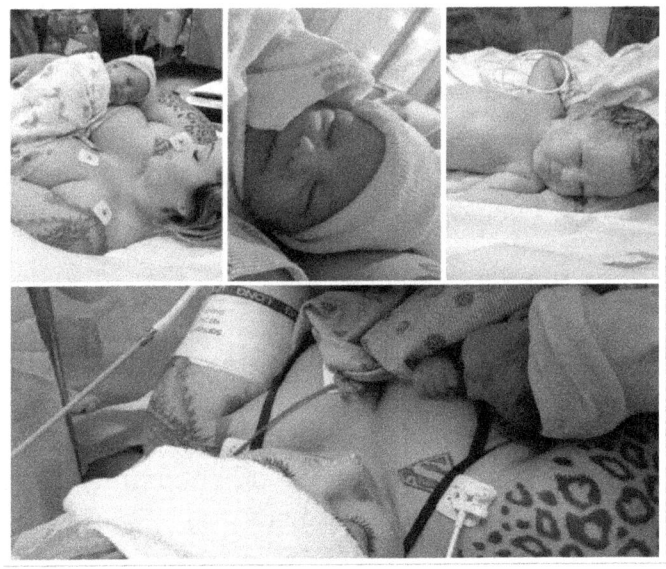

First Time Mom

Katie Theuer

Being a "first-time mom" I had no idea what to expect when I became pregnant. It was all new to me, and I wanted to hear other women's delivery stories! So I joined a "Due Date Group" for women due in May of 2016. I asked the women in this group so many questions about c-sections and delivery, and I appreciate all of the feedback I got from everyone! After the birth of my first child, I decided I would share my birth story, with the group that had helped me so much during my pregnancy journey. I ended up being in labor for 29 hours total and was +3, 10 cm, and 100% effaced when they told me I could start pushing.

I didn't have a lot of pressure or feeling of the baby's head being low, or that I needed to poop. I didn't even feel ready to push and I was expecting all of that! During my pregnancy, so many women had told me that's what would happen when I went into labor, but for me, it never really came! I only started pushing because they said it was time. When I started pushing, it felt like no matter what I did, she wasn't dropping low enough. Every time I pushed, she would get low, and they would say,

"We can see her brown hair!"

Then she would go back up until I pushed again and the nurse kept saying,

"One step forward, three steps back," after every push!

I had to work so hard to make any progress, and then the baby kept sliding back each time. I tried several different ways of pushing. I squatted using a bar, I was on my side, on my back, pulled myself up using a sheet tied around a pole; all sorts of ways! I was so exhausted from pushing, that I kept falling asleep in between contractions. My nurse was beyond amazing and was a total advocate for me! She knew I really wanted to try for a vaginal birth, to avoid a C-section if I could.

I kept crying because it felt like I wasn't making any progress; then the Dr. came into the room to say to me,

"You still have a ways to go, you need to push a good bit more."

After 3 hours of pushing, I knew they were getting close to talking about C-section, and I still didn't want to do that. My nurse said,

"I know your birth plan said, you weren't open to a vacuum."

My husband and I made a quick decision that if the Dr. felt it was safe, we would do it. She came back into the room and watched me push again to evaluate if I was close enough to use a vacuum. I pushed so hard! I literally started crying when the nurse said...

"Okay, yeah, let's do this! I can get her with the vacuum."

The Dr. and nurses explained to me that we've got three tries with the vacuum. If she didn't come out on the third try, we are automatically sent straight in for an emergency c-section. Dr. came back into the room, scrubbed up, and said:

"I need you to push harder than you have ever pushed now."

She inserted the vacuum, and I pushed so hard my baby girl's head came out! They told me her head was out, and they needed one more push, and then I'd be holding my daughter in my arms! One more push and my sweet girl had arrived!!! I ended up with an episiotomy along with 3rd-degree tears, which was not fun, but all so worth it to hold my sweet baby girl.

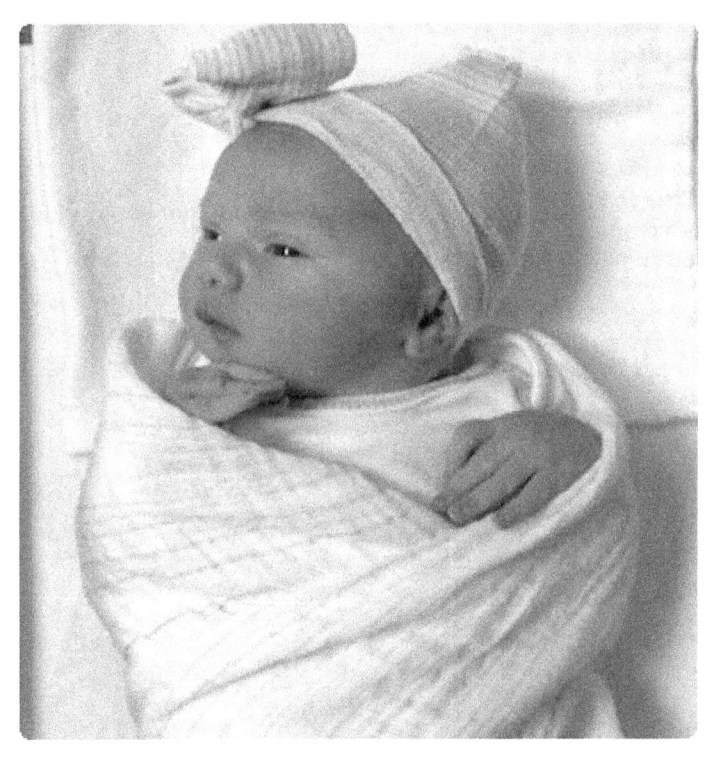

Austin Isabella
Date of Birth: May 4th, 2016
Birth Time:
Weight: 7 pounds 9 ounces
Height: 19 inches long

Katie Theuer

Katie Theuer

May 4, 2016

"We welcomed our sweet girl, Austin Isabelle Theuer, to the world today! 7 pounds 9 ounces and 19 inches! We are head over heels for her and so thankful!"

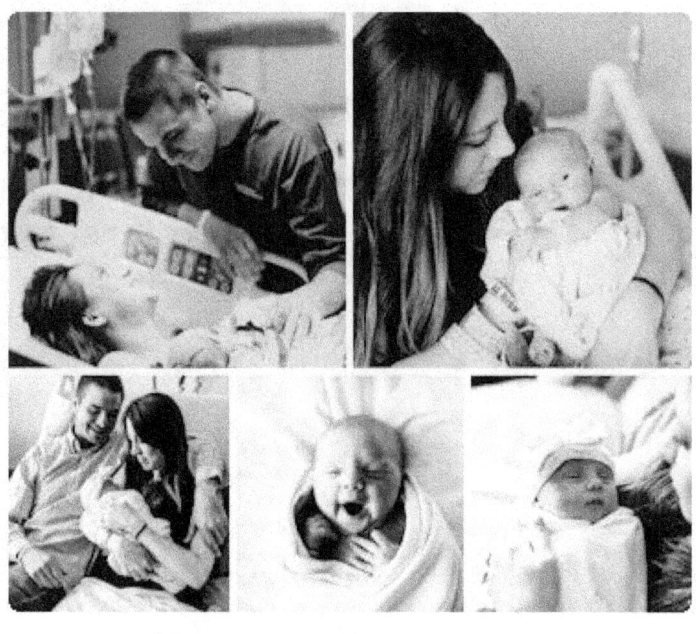

Our First Together

Tasha Crabb

I was pregnant with my second daughter; her due date was May 13th. She would be Derek's (my husband) first daughter, and our first child together. Well, I never made it to my due date, my doctor scheduled an induction for the 6th. I got up that morning, got myself ready, and proceeded to head to the hospital for my induction. It was set to begin at 6 am. The nurse started my IV and Pitocin right around 8 am. I felt like I was going to pass out! I think it was because of where the nurse put my IV. My contractions began almost immediately but were still tolerable. The doctor came into the room around 11 in the morning to check my cervix; I was 4-5 centimeters dilated and 70 percent effaced. Around 11:30-11:45 am the anesthesiologist came into my room to give me the epidural.

She must have hit a nerve or something because it felt like it was in my butt cheek. My whole body automatically jumped, and the anesthesiologist immediately began to yell at me to stay still! Once the epidural was in place, I was pretty much numb from the waist down. My doctor came back into the room and proceeded to break my water. The contractions became more intense after that. I could feel some pressure, but no pain. After a while, I began to feel the contractions, but only on my left side, so I pressed the button to get more medicine. I finally had relief again!

Around 3 pm, my nurse came back to do another cervical check. I was now 8-9 centimeters dilated and 80 percent effaced. Once 3:45, came around, I said...

"I feel like the baby is coming!"

The nurse told me, *"No, not yet!"*

I was just like, "Seriously, I need to push!!"

The nurse checked my cervix this time, and I was just shy of 10 centimeters, and 100 percent effaced. She said I just had a "little bit of lip" left. About 15 minutes later at 4 pm., I called the nurse back into the room to tell her,

"It's Time! The baby is coming NOW!!!"

The nurse went to get my doctor, and sure enough, I was right! She was already making her way out. The nurse told Derek to grab my legs and help me push because I was struggling to bare down. I was having horrible neck pain from the epidural. I had to force myself to bear down and push; only three pushes, and five minutes later she was born! There was no need for stitches, as I had no tearing. I was so in love with her! We did skin to skin for about an hour. Then they were ready to do her weight check and all of her measurements. When the nurses got done with her, they handed her back to me. I nursed her, and she did well at it. She was such a quiet baby. A few hours after giving birth, we went to the mommy and me suit to finish our stay in the hospital. Once we settled into our room, we got some dinner and cake. It was nice. Unfortunately, I ended up suffering from spinal headaches, which also caused me to have neck pain. I didn't sleep for the first four days after delivery. When I went home from the hospital, the headache seemed to get much worse. So, I ended up having to have a blood patch done.

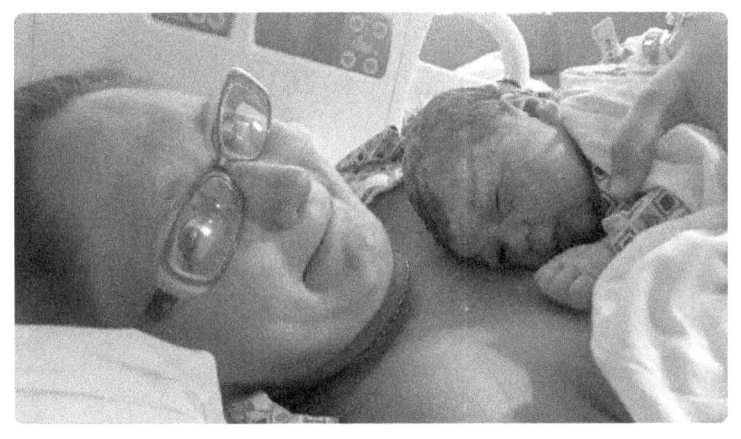

Karleigh
Date of Birth: May 6th, 2016
Birth Time:
Weight: 7 pounds 4 ounces
Height: 19½ inches

Tasha Crabb

Tasha Crabb

May 6, 2016

"Karleigh was born at 4:06 pm 7lbs 4oz 20.5in long I called all 3 on the head. She is the perfect baby and a boobie champ! I pushed for lit 5 min and she came flying out. No tears, no stitches nothing."

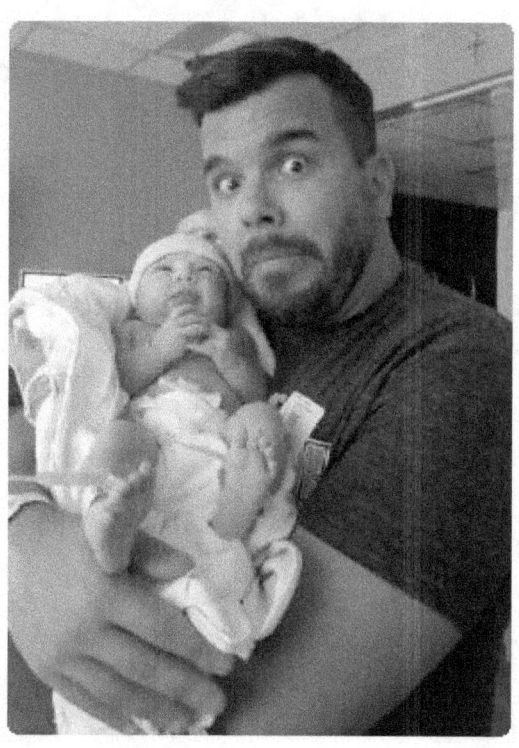

Lotus Birth

Thorn Tillson Epp

On May 10th, 2016, I had my last prenatal appointment. My due date had passed as I was due on May 8th. I had my membranes stripped that day, and I immediately began to notice contractions starting. They were consistent, but not yet painful, so later that day, I had my mom picked up my son because I knew labor was beginning. We went to bed early that night. In the morning, my husband and I decided to have sex to keep labor progressing; it had worked! My contractions had continued. I drew myself a bath so I could relax for a bit as my husband began filling our birthing pool. At this point, we felt no need to call my midwife. We then went back to bed, cuddled up, and watched some videos for about an hour. While hubby and I sat in bed eating our snacks, I began to notice my contractions were picking up and growing very painful. My husband rubbed my back for me, then said he would help me to the living room and make the call to my midwife. It was about an hour, or so later, before my midwife and her assistant arrived at our house.

 My midwife checked for dilation; I was 7 cm dilated. She told me I could relax in the pool if I wanted, so I did. I breathed through every contraction, but they began to slow down.

I then asked my midwife to break my waters, so she did, it wasn't going to be, long after, that the baby was here. I was back in the pool; it was time to start pushing. I only push for about 15 minutes. I was able to help catch Sage Gwenivere as she was being born, it was swift and almost painless. It felt amazing to finally hold her! She weighed just under seven and a half pounds, and she had a full head of hair. I was able to breastfeed her right away, and soon after, her dad was able to do skin on skin contact too! My husband was so happy to hold her; it brought him to tears. I later found out I was only in active labor 6 hours before my daughter was born. I had thought I was in labor for longer because my husband had told me she was born at 12, and I thought he meant am not pm. We chose not to cut the cord but let it naturally fall off on its own; it only took nine days. I found her birth very fulfilling and memorable, and I'm more in love with this sweet girl every day.

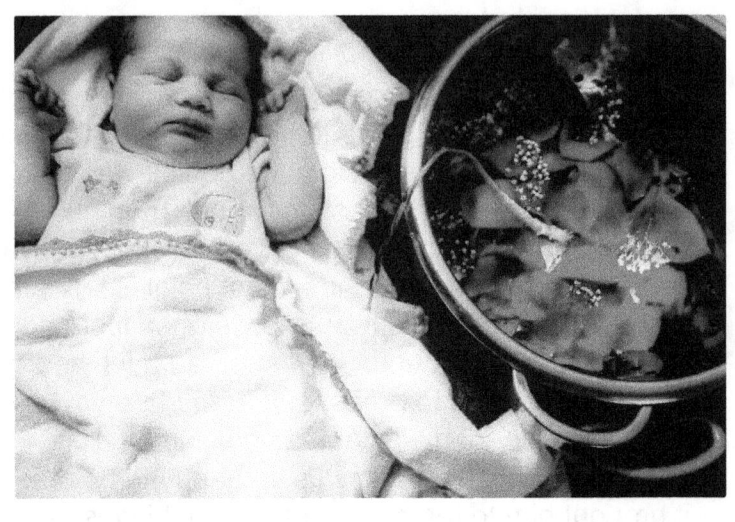

Sage Gwenivere
Date of Birth: May 11th, 2016
Birth Time: 12ish pm
Weight: 7 pounds ½ pounds
Height: N/A

Thorn Tillson Epp

Thorn Tillson Epp

May 11, 2016

"Here's Sage on daddy. I had a beautiful water birth, more photos soon to come!"

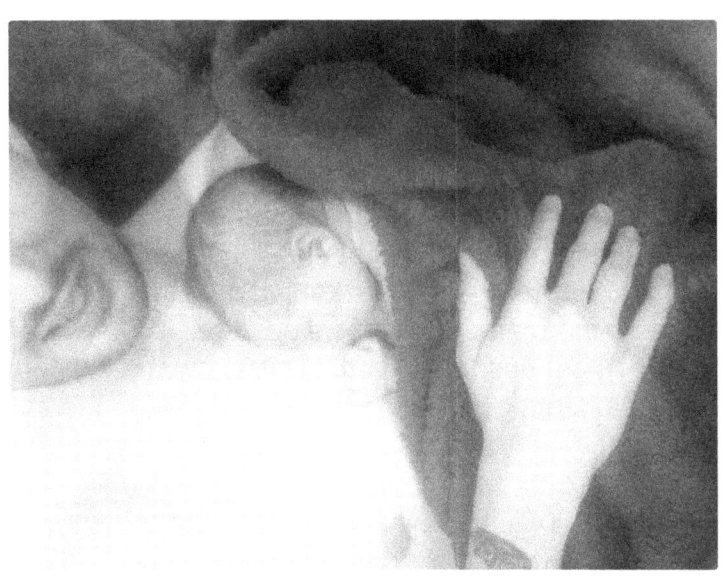

Birth Fear

Alicia Ward

On Thursday, May 5th, at 38 weeks and six days, I was having some cramping off and on all day. As the day progressed, the cramping seemed to intensify. After having Austin's dad and his fiancé Heather come over to visit, Heather and I went to get pedicures done. They wouldn't allow me to use the back massage and avoided pressure points during the foot massage. After that, we went to Walmart, where the cramping began to pick up. Heather and I grabbed some dinner and headed home. Once I got home, I decided to lay down and see if the cramping would stop. It felt like intense period cramps, along with terrible lower back pain. I had a heating pad on my back and decided to try to time the contractions. By what I was recording, they were 2-7 minutes apart and lasting varying amounts of time. I was pretty sure these were real contractions at this point, so I decided we had better, head to the hospital and see what was going on, it was about 8:30 pm. On the way to the hospital, I noticed every bump intensified the pain. Once I got to the hospital and was hooked up to the monitors, it was clear I was having contractions. Declan was doing great, and the contractions were only 3-4 minutes apart. After continuous monitoring and contacting my OB, they decided to admit me to the antenatal section for observation and IV fluids overnight. Once I was in a room, they started an IV with fluids and kept us hooked up to monitors. Contractions, heart, blood pressure, and pulse ox all night long. It was a long night, I got up every 1-2 hours to pee and had to have the nurse help me get hooked and unhooked each time. All the nurses at the hospital were terrific! They would tell me that they really hoped my doctor would go ahead and induce me; instead of making me wait one more day for my scheduled induction. (Saturday, May 7th.) The contractions weakened but continued all night long. The next morning I was still only 1 cm and had made no changes so they would not label me as being in labor. They blamed dehydration for the contractions. Once my Dr. finally came to see me, he decided to go ahead with the induction!

We were finally going to meet our boy! They brought me some breakfast to eat before the big event. It took until the afternoon to transfer me to my labor room and get things going. Once we got switched over, and everything was set up, we discussed the Foley Bulb to see how it would feel, how it works, etc. Since my cervix was so high and tender from being checked, they decided to give me some Nubain in my IV before inserting the foley bulb. They also had my antibiotics going at this point for being GBS, because I tested positive for it during a prenatal appointment. When they were inserting the foley bulb, it wasn't as uncomfortable as I thought it would be. It was, however, extremely awkward feeling having it hanging out of me! The foley bulb was inserted, at about 1:30 pm, the contractions started to become slightly stronger as I progressed. At about 3:30 pm, the nurse was checking on me and I kept telling her it felt like the foley bulb was slipping out. She checked and said it wasn't quite time, then went about checking my vitals. Suddenly I felt a small pop, and out it slid! That meant we were at 3 cm, and it was time to start Pitocin. I asked if I could do some walking to help things progress, and the nurse said,

"Once the Pitocin is hooked up, we prefer you to stay in the room so we can monitor you and the baby."

They let me walk for about 20 minutes before starting the Pitocin. Austin walked a few laps around the maternity floor with me, and then Heather walked a few. The contractions picked up slightly, but nothing major. Once I was back in the room, the nurse got the Pitocin hooked up, and Heather and I played some cards. It felt good to sit up and get out of the bed for a while, I ended up getting a bit sleepy, so I decided to lay down and take a nap. Not sure what time I woke up, or how long I napped, but the contractions were regular again, but still not painful. The Dr's came in and out, checking progression every so often; it was going incredibly slowly. Around midnight I was checked and still 3-4 cm. I was given two options.

Option 1:
I could stop the Pitocin, eat, and get some rest, and restart it in the morning.

Option 2:
I could keep chugging on.

I was exhausted and starving. Still, there was no way in hell was I stopping! Not when I was working so hard to get my baby out, so I was given a small dose of Nubain again for the pain, some Zofran for nausea, and a heating pad for my back. I was finally comfortable enough to take a nap. I went into a deep sleep for roughly an hour. At 1:15 am I woke from a night of deep sleep to a "POP!" Gush my water broke! It startled me, but I knew exactly what it was, despite being asleep. I instantly woke up and said,

"Oh! My water broke!"

Austin and I called the nurse, then I went to the bathroom while they got my bedding changed. Right about the time I got back into bed, my contractions started hitting super hard and fast. One on top of the other, and each one stronger than the one before. My nurse turned my Pitocin down, and I asked to go ahead and get the epidural. At 2 am, I got my epidural and was able to get some decent sleep. As of 9 am, I was still stuck at 4 cm. They said my membranes had only partially ruptured, so I went ahead and broke the rest of my waters. At this point, my contractions were powerful, and they had turned my Pitocin down to a four because my body almost entirely took over after my initial water breaking. At 10:30 am I was rechecked by one of the nurses, I was 5cm and 70% effaced, Declan was at a -1 station. I was happy with the progress, even if my labor was taking forever. At about 12:50 pm, I was still at 5cm, 90%, and -1 station. I had some Tylenol for the pain in my back muscles, from lying in bed continuously. The Dr. said once I was fully effaced, dilating would go quicker. At some point, I dozed back off, and around 1:30 pm the nurse came in, woke me up, and had me put on an oxygen mask. Declan's heart rate was dropping with each contraction. The oxygen mask helped, and he was staying stable. At 2:30 pm when the nurse was checking my vitals, we found I had a low-grade fever of 99.4. The nurse told me that we need to hurry up and get the baby out. At 2:50 pm, I was at 6cm. and they were keeping an extra close eye on both Declan and I. They had me keep the oxygen mask on at all times, for Declan's heart decelerations, which were still ok with the oxygen. I was starting to worry. I felt exhausted even though I had dozed off and on through my whole labor.

I started telling my Dr. he had better get my baby here and healthy, no matter how he had to do it! About 3:15 pm, my Dr. came in to check me and said I was at 7cm. The nurses started giving me extra IV fluid because Declan was now having tachycardia episodes. Where his heart would race in the 180s-190s, and he would move around a ton. My doctor changed me to a stronger antibiotic and said Declan and I were still ok for now. At 4 pm, my temp was at 99.1, and they decided to continue waiting and watching us closely. At 5 pm I was checked and at 8cm. I asked them to turn the epidural down slightly because both my legs were so numb I couldn't move them on my own at all. Once the epidural came down, I started feeling a lot of pain in my cervix and asked for it to be, bumped back up. It all took place over a couple of hours, but I couldn't tell you exactly when things were starting to get rough for me physically. At some point, the nurse checked me, because I told her I was feeling pressure, she said I was still at 8cm. Right after that, I started feeling extremely nauseous. I asked for Zofran, and they gave it to me, but not fast enough. I started throwing up, having chills, and feeling like crap. After 15 minutes of vomiting, they gave me a second dose of Zofran. I felt like all my senses were overloaded, I wanted to keep my eyes closed, and didn't want to see, hear, or feel anything. The nurse rechecked me again and said I was still at 8cm.

My husband kept trying to gently rub my leg or touch me to calm me down, and I kept telling him,

"Don't touch me!"

If a nurse or doctor asked me anything, the only response I was able to give a thumbs up or down. Then, I felt my body start pushing with each contraction. And I felt his head right there. I told the nurse that I couldn't fight the pushing. I felt his head she argued with me that she had just checked and I was still only 8 cm then, my doctor came in, and he asked if I was pushing and I told him not voluntarily and that I felt the baby's head. He checked me and said,

"Well, I see why you're pushing, the baby is crowning! It's baby time!"

The room suddenly filled with people getting things prepared. The nurse had me start doing practice pushes with her at around 7:45 pm and by eight, my doctor was ready to go, and we were doing the real pushing. I felt like I was pushing with everything I had in me for so long. The nurses kept saying I was doing great! I could feel Declan's nose coming out! It seemed so distinct, then the next thing I knew everyone was screaming,

"PUSH! PUSH!! PUSH!!! PUSH!!!! PUSH!!!!!", with no stopping, in-between time.

I heard my doctor say to grab the Vacuum Extractor. I listened to the vacuum pop off of his head twice. While one Dr. was using the vacuum, another was reaching into me, pulling on my son, and a nurse was shoving him down through my belly. No one was telling what was going on, I was so scared, I thought we had lost his heartbeat or the cord was around his neck. No one was saying anything, then I finally felt it his body slide out like a fish. He was born at 8:28 pm after 15 minutes of practice pushes, and 30 minutes of really pushing. There was no crying, no one said anything, no one told me until days after his birth that he was born entirely blue from the shoulders up, and the rest of his body was grey. We nearly lost him! I saw Austin cut the cord, and they rushed Declan over to work on him. I kept saying,

"What's wrong?! Why isn't he crying?!"

No one would tell me what was going with my son. After a couple of minutes, I started to hear him make a raspy, wheezy noise. I don't know what his first Apgar Test was, but his second was only 6.

I was so focused on what was going on with my baby, I didn't even tell the doctor that I could feel him as the stitches were being put in, but I didn't care. I only had two stitches, but both were long. The one on the right side, and one at the bottom. The Doctors finally got Declan stabilized and rushed him to the NICU. I kept asking everyone what was going on, and they told me a NICU doctor would be in to talk with us. Finally, she came in and talked to us, after what felt like forever. Declan's lungs were slightly underdeveloped, like that of a preemie. The sound he was making was him trying to breathe, but he couldn't because the lungs were still sticking together. He was also acting just like a baby, of a mom who had GD. She told us he was on CPAP to open his airway; it was at 30% oxygen. They had an IV in and were giving him some sugar water and antibiotics. His blood sugar was 30, and they want it at 50. They wanted to do a central line because it's hard to get a suitable vein in a chubbier baby. When he was born, he was very stressed, and his heart rate was in the 230s. It was still high, in the 190s and they weren't sure why. They told us it was touchy and they didn't know if Declan would improve or decline. My doctor. said he would be sending out my placenta for testing because of the fever I developed during labor. I was told I could not get out of bed for 2 hours because of the epidural, and I would be taken to see Declan at that time. Austin was not able to see Declan; they said they would come and get us when they knew more. It was the scariest time of my life. Finally, at 10:40 pm, a NICU doctor came to talk to us. Declan had improved and he wanted to start to wean him off the oxygen overnight.

His heart rate was in the 150s now because of the fever I had, so they wanted him on antibiotics for 48 hours, until we knew for sure he did not have the infection. He told us Declan was moving his right arm and hand fine, was not sure of his left, and he had shoulder dystocia. Shortly after seeing the NICU doctor we were finally taken to meet our son. It was so scary to see him covered in IV's, CPAP, and Monitors, but he was the most beautiful baby I had ever seen. I just sat and touched him through the incubator until they sent us back to our room. It was impossible to sleep that night; I just wanted my baby. We were back in the NICU first thing the next morning; I was told I would get to hold him that day and couldn't wait! I finally got to hold him skin to skin, that afternoon. We were also told we could try feeding him in the evening. He graduated from the CPAP that afternoon. He was improving with leaps and bounds, and we were going to try nursing in the evening! He had a feeding tube down his nose, and we had Heather bring my frozen expressed colostrum to feed him. The NICU was terrific. I slowly gave him the colostrum through the feeding tube as we nursed so that he would associate nursing with a full belly.

He was an excellent nurser from the start, latched and sucked just great! I started making sure to be at the NICU on a strict 3-hour schedule for feedings so that I could nurse every feed and then would pump in my room after each session. It was exhausting.

When I came to do his 6 am, feed he had graduated from the isolette into an open crib. We were able to put some clothes on him! The Dr. said he was doing fantastic; he was surprised he was doing so well. If Declan continued to nurse well, we would remove the feeding tube, and the IV's would come out after. He would prove he could keep his blood sugar levels steady on his own based on exclusively breastfeeding. Every minute was focused on being in the NICU, holding and feeding him, and pumping. By that night, the feeding tube was gone. He was nursing like a champ, and he finally got rid of the IVs! Our boy was nearly wire-free, and when holding him, he was able to be detached from the monitors. When I came for Declan's early morning feed around 6 am, I was told there was a possibility of him going home the next day. He would need to continue to keep his blood sugar levels maintained and continue doing well with nursing. The day was again spent focusing on feeding and pumping. Finally, that Tuesday morning, we found out that Declan was strong enough and doing well enough to come home with mommy! He had his circumcision done, and we did our discharge class that included mommy and daddy giving him a sponge bath. It was a hectic day, and he was struggling with nursing due to sleepiness. He was given pumped milk through a bottle once and nursed once. By the time we were being discharged, I was worried that he wasn't taking enough in, so the nurse brought in a little formula, and we gave him ½ oz through the bottle before leaving. He had my pumped milk by syringe at home that night when he continued to refuse the breast. Overnight he started nursing great again, and here we are! My milk is in and my son is doing excellent! Now, as far as Declan goes, he does have some lasting issues due to the roughness of his birth. He still has a very sore, swollen knot on his head from the vacuum. It's going down slowly, but still going to be painful for him. He also has a brachial plexus shoulder injury. He does not move his left arm at all. Declan could move his fingers/wrist slightly, but they were fragile. The doctors had us keep his left arm safely pinned in a sling position to prevent the shoulder from moving around. We saw an orthopedic specialist on Friday, the 20th of 2017. Overall, we had an extremely traumatic birth. Still, Declan's big brother is his guardian angel, somehow he pulled through, and I'm so thankful to have such a strong, healthy, little boy! I also found out later that when my doctor came in and asked if I was pushing, he was coming in to take me for a cesarean. Still, when he checked, and the baby was crowning, he didn't feel comfortable waiting.

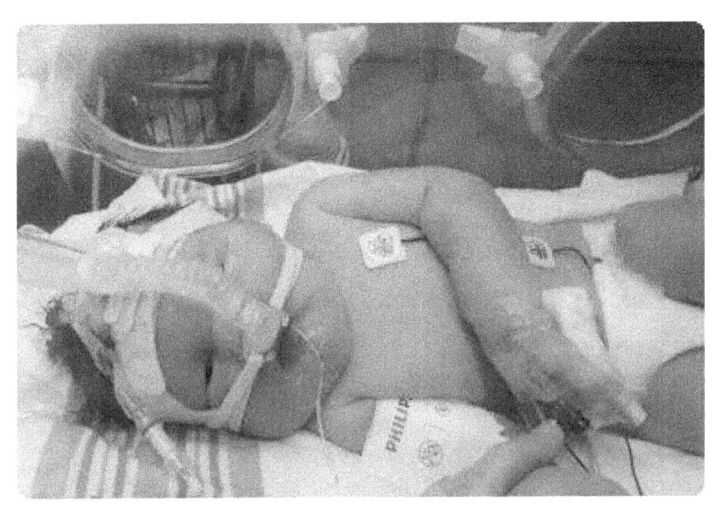

Declan
Date of Birth: May 7th, 2016
Birth Time: 8:35 pm
Weight: 9 pounds 9.2 ounces
Height: 20⅞ inches

Alicia Ward

Alicia Ward

May 5, 2016

"I'm At l&d. They are real contractions, not sure how far apart but they have slowed since leaving home. Bp was high, checking blood and urine for pre-eclampsia. I'm 1cm dilated."

Alicia Ward

May 6, 2016

"39-week pic"

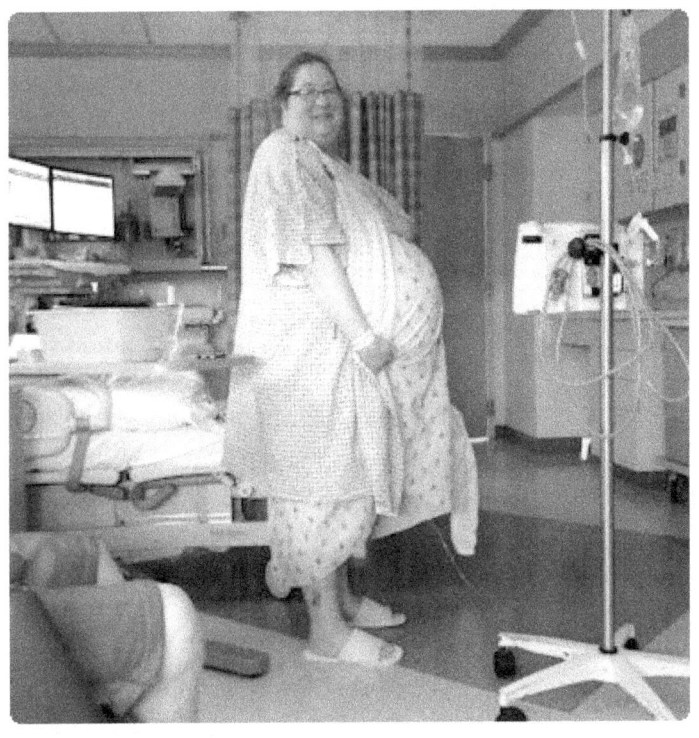

Alicia Ward

May 8, 2016

"Finally, I got to see my handsome little man. He is just perfect! He has daddy's forehead and my nose. Long curly hair, still matted so can't tell color yet! Super long toes. He's a bit bruised from being stuck. His stats are excellent right now. He is on CPAP, has an iv for antibiotics and glucose. He's doing great. Opened his eyes for us a few times. And I can settle his cries with my touch and voice. They said I should be able to hold him tomorrow, it broke my heart to leave him in there but I will go back and see him one more time before I sleep tonight, I'm finally about to eat and they are getting me about pump so I can start pumping for him. He weighs 9lbs 9.2oz and is 20 7/8in long!"

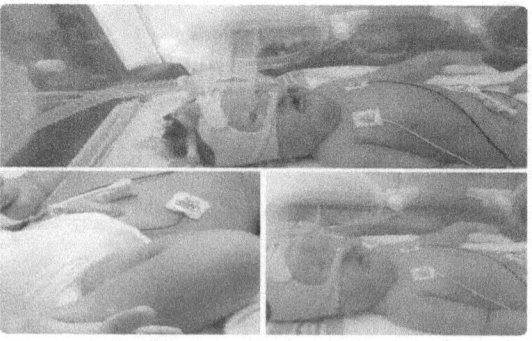

Alicia Ward

May 9, 2016

"Update on my big NICU baby: He is off CPAP, feeding tube removed, and slowly weaning off IV. Out of the incubator and into the open crib. We are now nursing on demand and doing sticks to check his blood sugar, as long as he continues to nurse well and maintains his blood sugar, he can go home as soon as tomorrow or Wednesday!!!! Just got a good 12 mins on the right, and 25 on the left! He must be getting something because he is sound asleep and content."

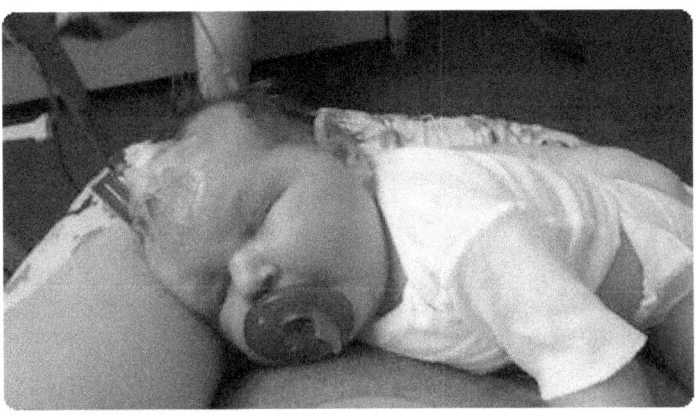

"Neonatal Brachial Plexus Injuries "Brachial Plexus Injury," is a common birth injury, and occurs in one to three out of every 1,000 births in the United States. The nerves of the Brachial Plexus can stretch, compress, or tear under challenging deliveries. The result can be a loss of muscle function or even paralysis to the upper arm of the child."

For more information on Neonatal Brachial Plexus Injuries, please check out the website provided below.

https://kidshealth.org/en/parents/brachial-plexus.html

High Pressure

Bethany Adkins

Suzy's original due date was May 27th, 2016. Since I had an emergency c-section in my previous pregnancy with my son, I was scheduled for a repeat c-section on May 20th. I had issues throughout my entire pregnancy, from my blood pressure to excruciating migraines, due to preeclampsia. After having a migraine for four days with no relief, I finally decided to go to the hospital on May 12th. Upon arriving at the hospital, I went directly to labor and delivery to be monitored. While being monitored, my blood pressure was higher than usual. After being there for two hours, my blood pressure shot up to 220/208! At this point, my doctor decided that I would no longer be pregnant. That today was the day my daughter was to be born and immediately, due to hypertension in my pregnancy. The situation was becoming life-threatening to both me and my unborn child. I was quickly taken and prepared for another emergency c-section. The anesthesiologist came into the operating room and administered an epidural, so I could be awake during the birth. It was unlike my previous experience. After thirty minutes I welcomed Suzanne- Elizabeth Victrice Adkins to the world.

She was born at 11:19 pm on May 12th, 2016. Weighing 8 pounds 15 ounces and measuring 18 inches long. I was able to hold my daughter immediately after delivery, while the doctor was still stitching me back up. Also, unlike my previous c-section with my son, we ended up only having to spend three days in the hospital, before being released on the 15th.

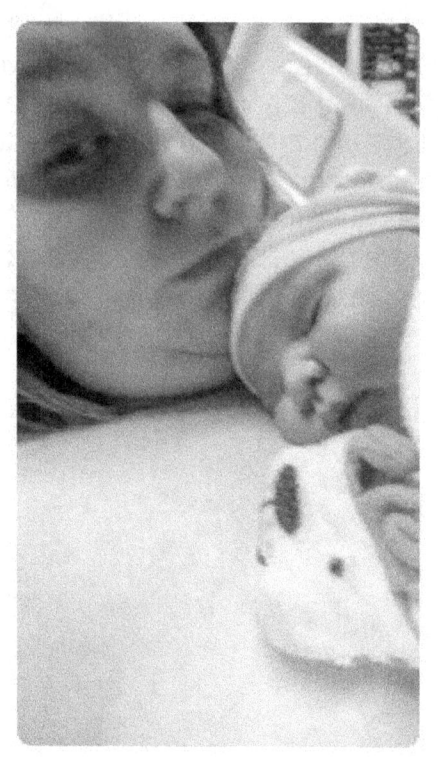

Suzanne-Elizabeth Victrice
Date of Birth: May 12th, 2016
Birth Time: 11:19 pm
Weight: 8 pounds 15 ounces
Height: 18 inches

Bethany Adkins

All Natural

Shayla Kieneker

I was scheduled to be induced on May 13th at 5:45 am, I was 40 weeks and 5 days! My Doctor told me at my last appointment, might as well get him on out of there. On May 12th, my fiance, my mom and I took a 2-mile walk and had a picnic to try and induce my labor naturally. At 9:30 pm on the 12th, I was "cramping" but ignored it and went to bed, only to wake up at 12:30 am and realize they were contractions, that were 5 minutes apart. I called L and D and was told to come on in. We got to the hospital at 1:20 am, and my mom showed up 5 minutes behind us. I was only 3cm dilated at that time, and 2 hours later I had only made it to 5cm dilated, and in lots of pain from contractions. My nurse finally decided to give me Fentynol in my IV to help with the pain. Once I was at 7cm, my new nurse came in and said she would see about getting me an epidural. I waited for 20 minutes before the nurse, and my doctor came back and said,

"We're sorry you can't have that, epidural."

Apparently, if your blood platelets are too low, you're not allowed to have one done.

So, I delivered Troy Greyson 3 hours later naturally once the Doctor had broken my water. I pushed for 20 minutes, and there he was. I never planned to deliver naturally, but I definitely felt proud of myself for doing it. I didn't cry once or complain about the pain, I just pushed until he was here. My fiance said I turned into the Hulk during the pushing! He also said he'll never mess with me again!

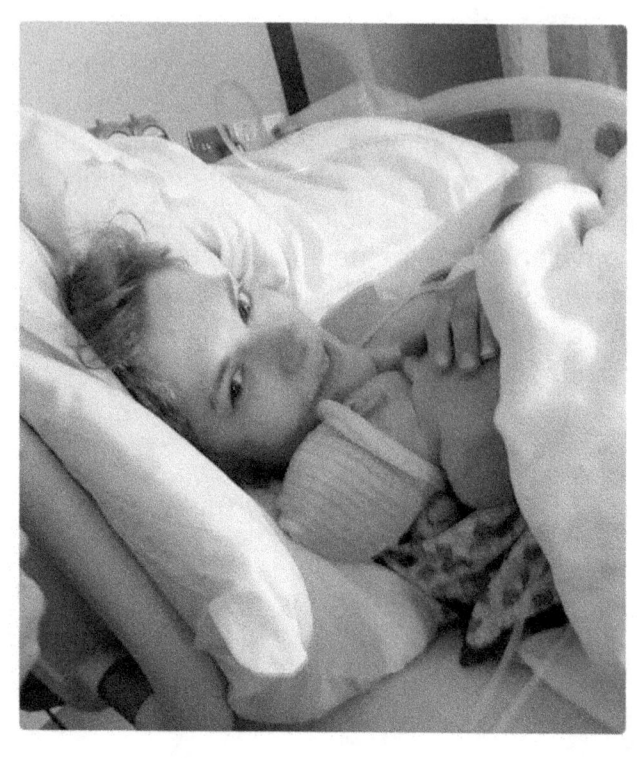

Troy Greyson
Date of Birth: May 13th, 2016
Birth Time: 2:06 pm
Weight: 6 pounds 14 ounces
Height: 19 ½ inches

Shayla Kieneker

Shayla Kieneker

May 15, 2016

"Troy Greyson Merrifield, born Friday the 13th at 2:06 pm, with no epidural so I'm in a bit of pain. 6 pounds 14 ounces and 19 and 1/2 inches. I pushed for 20 minutes before we got to meet him. #SoInLove"

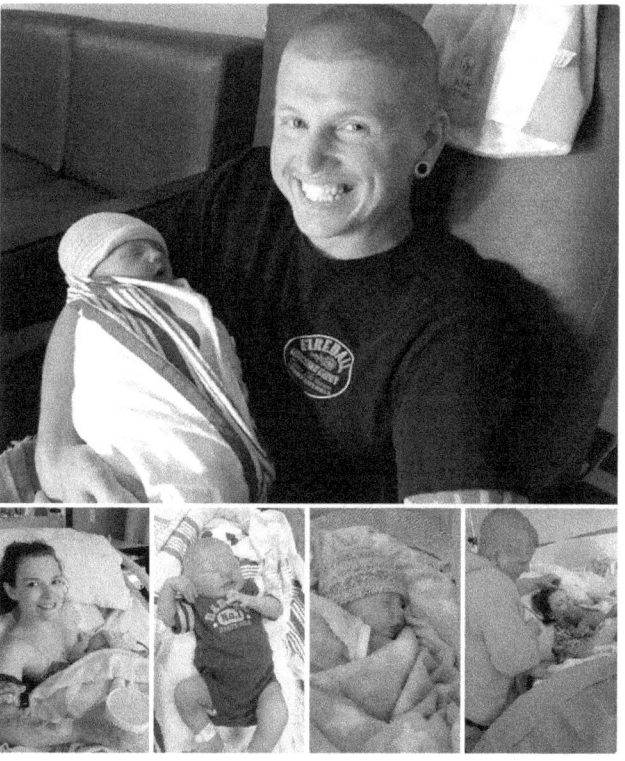

NICU

Danielle Bair

I woke up, Saturday, May 14th, at 5:15 am, with very consistent contractions. I just laid in bed and timed them for a while; I decided to wake hubby up about 15 minutes later. After about an hour they were 4 minutes apart, so I called my doctor and headed to the hospital. It was about 7 am at this point, and contractions were painful but still tolerable. The doctor came in and checked me, and I was only 2 cm and 80%. He kept me in triage for another 2 hours and rechecked me for progression. NOTHING! Still 2cm and 80%, so I was sent home. It was about 2 pm now, because of the traffic. Pretty much as soon as I got home, the contractions got 1000 times worse. I tried laying in bed, I tried laying down in the bath, I also tried walking, but nothing was helping with the intense pain. The pain became so bad that it started to make me physically ill. I was vomiting with every contraction, so I made a choice to go back at 4 pm. I get there and the doctor checks me, still no progression, but because of my pain, an IV catheter was placed, and I was given Stadol and Zofran. Two hours later, he rechecks me; I was 2 1/2 cm 80%. The doctor doesn't want to send me home in this much pain, so he decides to do another check in an hour.

An hour later, he comes in and checks me, and I can tell by his face there still has been no change, and I swear he lied that I was 3cm now so that he could admit me. Flash forward, finally getting admitted and transferred to my delivery room, the anesthesiologist comes in and the epidural is placed. Finally, I can sleep. 11:30 pm rolls around and the doctor comes in to check me, I'm 4cm. He decides to break my water, and my husband almost passes out. Fast forward again to about 1:45 am on the 15th now. The doctor comes in and checks me... 8cm and 100%! My hubby called and told my mom to get to the hospital, asap! My actual OB comes in and I was so happy to see her, she's also my family doctor. It was about twenty minutes later when she checked me, and I was now 9 cm and having a horrid urge to start pushing. Then, the baby's heart rate began to drop with every contraction. Even though the baby was still in the -2 station, she said I could start. He needed to come out soon! So I'm bearing down with my contractions, as well as pushing in between to get baby in 0 stations. After an hour of pushing, I was so close to giving up, because I was physically and mentally exhausted. My doctor tells me she can feel his hair, and then tells me to push as hard as I ever have before! Finally, he was so close to coming out! I had to stop pushing at that point so she could gown up for the catch, and get me in the stirrups! It was the hardest part of that whole night.

Two pushes later, they flopped my son on my belly. I don't know what I felt at that moment other than,

"Holy shit, I just had a baby."

Hubby cut the cord quickly because it was around his neck, and they immediately rushed him over to be checked because he wasn't crying. Hubby stayed with me while they took him to keep me calm, and my mom went with the baby. Twenty minutes later, (seemed like a year) they bring him back to me.

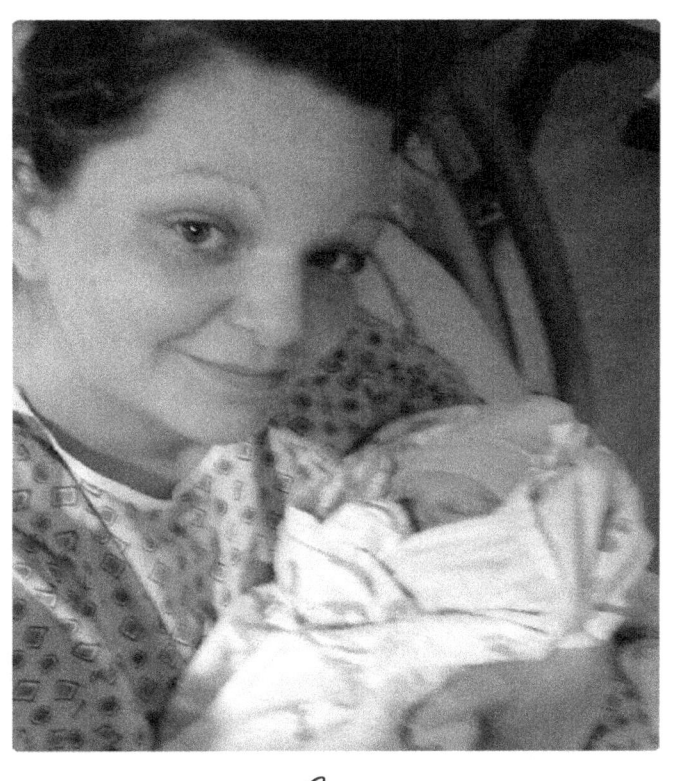

Cooper
Date of Birth: May 15th, 2016
Birth Time: 3:16 am
Weight: 6 pounds 1 ounce
Height:

Danielle Bair

Danielle Bair

May 16, 2016

"Just some pictures that were taken after epidural and birth. I miss my little man so much."

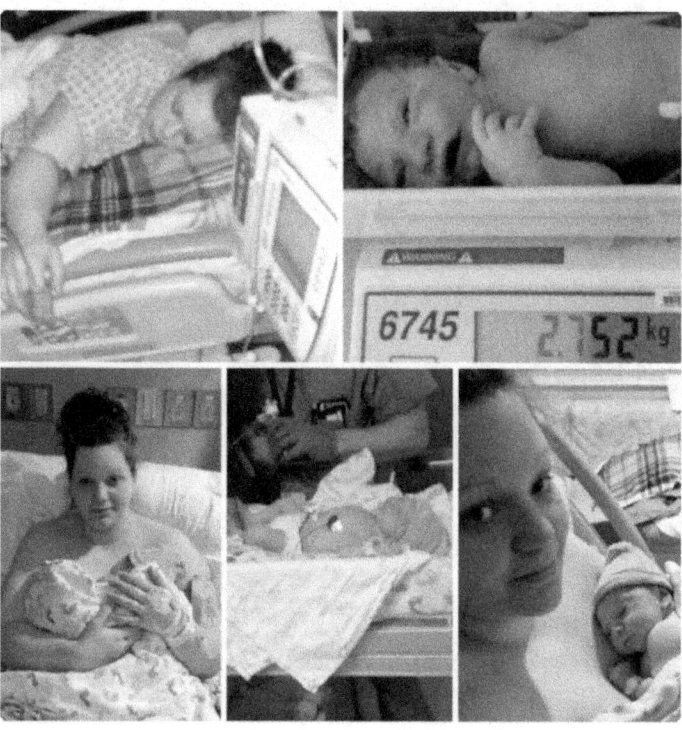

Danielle Bair

May 16, 2016

"Update on cooper. He has the start of a lung infection most likely caused by meconium in the sac before birth. He had to stay in the NICU for 48 hours, and they are discharging me today. I don't want to leave without him."

The Midwife

Jessica Pataky

I had been with my boyfriend for 5 years before we decided to start trying to conceive. It took us 9 months to finally get pregnant. Evelyn Leigh Leroux was due on May 16, 2016. On Sunday, May 15, I woke up and was feeling crampy. All-day I had cramps. Around 8 pm, the cramps were turning into contractions but were far from painful and weren't consistent. I decided to go to bed at around 10 pm, but I couldn't lie down because my contractions started coming quickly and fiercely. They were about 5 minutes apart and lasting close to a minute each. My midwife told me that I shouldn't call her until I could no longer handle the pain, or I would have to return home if I went too early. So, for 2 hours I danced around my living room with the contractions, which were all in my back, while my boyfriend slept in bed. At around midnight, I called Emma, my midwife, and she said she would come over to my house to check me before deciding if we should go to the hospital. She arrived at around 12:30 am and she had me lay on a towel in my bed and checked my cervix between contractions. They were coming one after another, and very consistent. The pain was probably at around a 5, I was 4cm dilated and had not yet lost my mucus plug.

We decided to go to the hospital right away so I could soak in the bath. The drive to the hospital was horrible, It was hurting me so bad to sit, and with every contraction, I wanted to get up off the seat. The pain was shooting through my back and hips. I texted my mom and my mother in law to let them know we were on our way to having a baby. My mom said she'd get up and come if I wanted her to, so I said she could. We arrived at the hospital at about 1:45. When I got there, I had to check-in at the ER, and all the staff kept trying to get me to sit in the wheelchair, but I couldn't sit for another second.

I needed to stand and sway. Finally, after so many contractions, I made it down the hall to the elevator, and into the labor and delivery room. A nurse came to take my blood, as I am Rh negative and needed a Rhogam injection, because my boyfriend is Rh-positive, and so is the baby. The baby can be positive or negative, but being positive would mean I need the injection. As soon as the nurse was finished, Emma rechecked my cervix, and I was 7 cm dilated by then. I undressed, got into the bathtub and turned on the jets. I couldn't get comfortable because, in order for a jet to hit me in the back where I needed it to, the jet in front of me would hit me in the vagina, and it was just annoying me!

I gave up and got out of the tub. When I got out, I had to pee, but as soon as I sat down it felt like I had to poop. Emma told me not to push while on the toilet because she didn't want the baby to be born on the toilet of course! At this time, my mom had shown up. Emma rechecked me again, and I was fully dilated. Woohoo!! My next contractions were different, and I needed to push!! I was standing beside the bed, leaning on it while my mom and boyfriend took turns squeezing my hips to help with the pain. After a couple of contractions, my legs started getting weak, and I wanted to squat.

Emma couldn't see it, so she asked me to get up on the bed. I got on the bed and was kneeling on all fours and could feel the head push out with every push, but when I stopped pushing, the baby went back up. It was pretty infuriating because I was working so hard to get the baby out. Still, she was being stubborn, haha. I changed positions and was lying on my side with my leg up to my chest. The contractions sorta slowed down, and I wasn't feeling the need to push anymore, but I didn't want to give up. I put my hand down and I could feel her there crowning. It felt squishy, so I forced myself to push, even though the contractions weren't as strong. Finally, Emma said one more big push, then pant pant pant. I felt a big gush of fluid hit my feet as the baby came out. It was my water breaking!

The baby was almost born en caul. Emma placed Evelyn on my belly and told me her cord wasn't long enough for her to reach my chest. This was when they told me she scored a 9/10 on the APGAR test. After about 5 or so minutes, the cord had stopped pulsing and was done doing its job, so she clamped it and Daddy cut it. He said it felt rubbery. Then she was brought up to my chest, and everything was right in the world. Evelyn Leigh Leroux was born at 3:41 am, the morning of her due date. Emma gave me the shot of Pitocin to help the placenta come out. After about 10 minutes, it came out with one small push. I needed two stitches in my perineum, so they froze me, and I swear that burned and hurt more than when the baby was coming out. The stitches didn't hurt, though I could feel the thread tugging and pulling, it was a weird feeling. After I was cleaned up, they placed warm blankets on me because I was shivering. I wasn't cold though, my body was in shock, I was told it was very common. Evelyn nursed reasonably well, and after a couple of hours, I passed her off to Daddy, so I could get cleaned up. She weighed 7 lbs, 9 ounces and was 19.5 inches long. Daddy was able to put her first diaper on, It took a couple of tries before it was on correctly. She again scored 9 on her APGAR Test, she was perfect. At 7 am, I was discharged and we were able to go home as a family of 3.

As we walked out of the hospital, it started to snow (in May) it only lasted a couple of minutes, and it was beautiful.

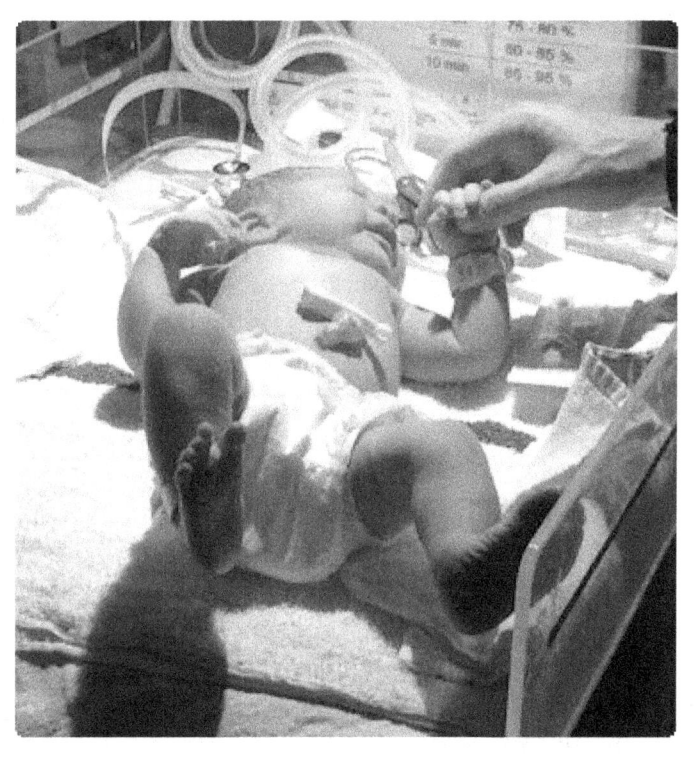

Evelyn Leigh Leroux
Date of Birth: May 16th, 2016
Birth Time: 3:41 am
Weight: 7 lbs 9 ounces
Height: 19 ½ inches long

Jessica Pataky

The Birth Of Ezekiel

Brandi Long Walter

With Ezekiel, everything happened so quickly! I went to the doctor's office that day with light contractions. The doctor told me to call him when I was ready to have a baby, but he said it would be that day for sure. I told him I'd like to wait at least till hubby got home from work. When my husband got home, he got showered, and we took the older two kids to my mothers-in-law, stopped at Turkey Hill to grab some snacks, and called to tell the doctor to head to the hospital. When I got to the hospital, the nurse kept arguing with me that I wasn't in labor, because how could I be if I wasn't freaking out and panicking from my contractions. I told the nurse I could feel them, and they were close but not super painful. So, she finally hooked me up to the monitor and was really impressed by my coolness with my contractions. She still kept trying to say that I should be at home, but I knew with how quick my last child came, the doctor didn't want me at home.

So he came in around 9 to check me, and I was like 5 or 6 centimeters dilated. He wanted me on an antibiotic. He said he'd break my water after the antibiotic ran for at least an hour. My doctor put me on the pit at this point and around 11 he came back and broke my water. At around 12, I told hubby I needed to sit up. He helped me sit up, at which point I screamed that I needed to push and to lay me down. Hubby starts freaking out because Ezekiel's crowning and no one was in the room. He runs to the hall as the nurse was coming in, she said she recognized my shriek. Doctor struts in all high and mighty, telling me not to push, as I tell him I'm not it's my body pushing. Ezekiel was born literally, within seconds after the doctor put his robe and gloves on. My doctor wouldn't allow us delayed cord clamping, and there wasn't much time for me to hold Ezekiel after he was born, as he needed to stitch me up right away. I kept telling the doctor I could feel the needle as he was stitching me, he would then tell me that I was lying about feeling the needle until he "tested" me. Finally, I was given more novocaine, which took the edge off, but I could still feel it! I've never seen that doctor again. He never checked on me through the night; I saw another doctor from the office the next morning around 9 am.

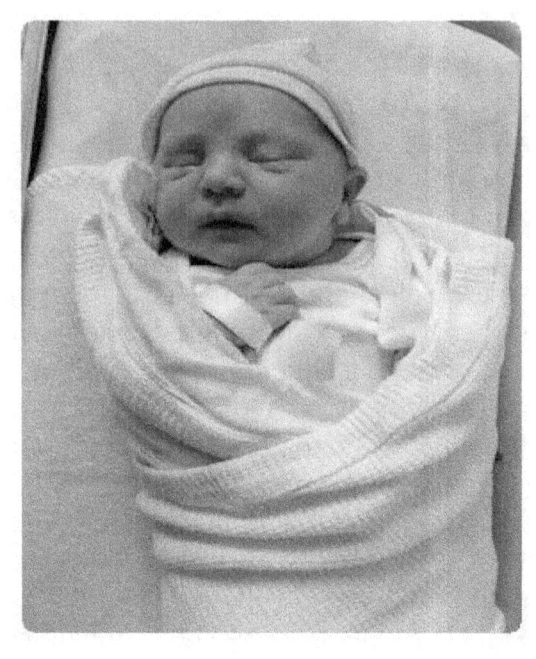

Ezekiel Guy
Date of Birth: May 18th, 2016
Birth Time: 12:12 am
Weight: 8 pounds 4 ounces
Height: 19½ inches

Brandi Long Walter

Beez Homemade on Facebook
bwalter88@icloud.com

My 5th Child

Ashley Franklin

It was Tuesday; May 17th when I had just gotten home from taking my son to his check-up at the pediatrician's office. I had my doctor's appointment the day before and was told if I didn't go into labor on my own, I was going to be induced the following week. So, hubby and I dropped my son off and left the kids with their big brother. Then went to the store around 5 pm, which is where I first started to notice I was having real contractions. We came home from the store, and I started dinner, but hubby had to finish cooking because the contractions were already getting bad. I just felt icky down there in my lady parts. I went to the bathroom, and sure enough, I was having a bloody show. I gathered my stuff together and quickly took a shower. My husband brought me dinner, so I tried to eat because I wasn't going to be able to eat again until after having Riley. Still, the pain was becoming too much for me to handle, so we headed to Labor and Delivery around 8 pm. When I got to the hospital, they sent me to a room to monitor me, to see if I was going to stay. At first, the nurse said I was only a 2 maybe 2 ½, she was going to check the chart to be sure. When she came back I was 4 cm and 70% effaced, so I would be staying until I had the baby. When I got to the labor & delivery room, I got my IV hooked up and only waited for about 30 minutes for the anesthesiologist to give me the epidural. It was about 9 pm or a little after, and I'm finally starting to get comfortable. My dad had texted me earlier that night, so I decided to text him back since I hadn't talked to him in months. I told him that I was going to have Riley and that I wanted him to meet my kids, (six years and five kids and at this point, he never met any of my children) but I don't hear from him again for more than 2 weeks. The nurse comes back in around 11-11:30 pm and checks me but I haven't had much progress, so I take a nap while I can. The nurse comes in again about 3 am or maybe a little before, to check my cervix. Now it was go time! She calls the doctor in, they get everything set up to deliver Riley, and it's time for me to start pushing. My water still hasn't broken yet, so the doctor says she wants me to try to deliver the baby inside the amniotic sac. I pushed a few times and she's halfway out now, you can see her shoulders. She's still in the sac, but when the doctor tries to turn her a little, the sac busts. Riley was born just moments later. The doctor said that Riley was the closest she had ever come to delivering a baby still in the amniotic sac.

I feel like if I could have just pushed with no help, she would have come with the sac still intact.

Then it was time to deliver my afterbirth, and the doctor told me that my placenta had torn into two pieces, so she had to make sure she cleaned everything out well. Riley was in my arms and breastfeeding within minutes of being born, and she latched on like a pro. She was so beautiful, and I loved her even more at every glance! Riley was born at 3:12 am on May 18th, 19 1/2in long, and weighed 7lb 15oz.

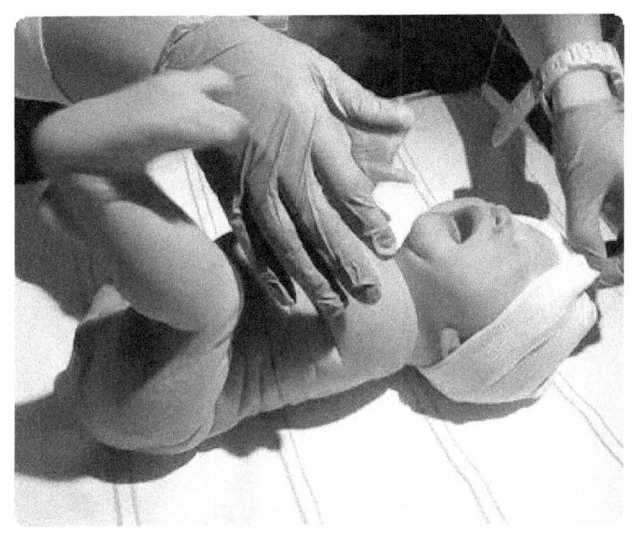

Riley Marie
Date of Birth: May 18th, 2016
Birth Time: 3:12 am
Weight: 7 pounds 15 ounces
Height: 19½ inches

Ashley Franklin

Ashley Franklin

May 17, 2016

"I'm in L&D, I got my epidural, dilated 5cm, and my bag is bulging."

Ashley Franklin

May 19, 2016

"My daughters came to see me and Riley in the hospital tonight since we don't get discharged until tomorrow. Riley started crying while my oldest girl was holding her and she started singing twinkle twinkle little star to her. All on her own too! I love my kids so much!!!"

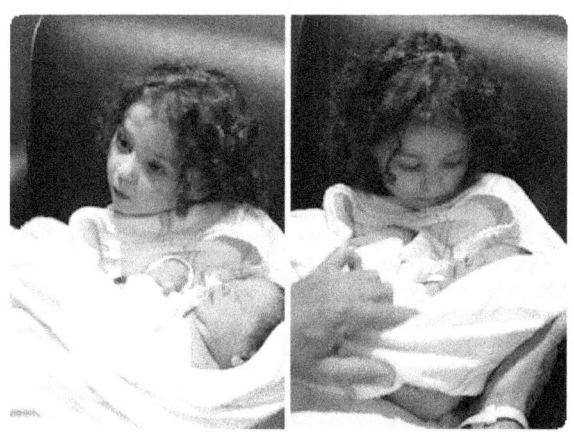

My Third and Last

Bailey Nicole Kemper

My daughter Silvia was my third and last pregnancy. My pregnancy with her was completely different from my other pregnancies. She was the first girl! During my entire pregnancy, I had never-ending morning sickness. I did, however, break out with horrible acne that never went away. Everything swelled up, and I've never had that happen before. I had false contractions constantly. But Silvia was a repeat c section, my third. The day I had Silvia, was a normal one. I dropped my oldest off at school, dropped my second off at grandma's house, and then drove to the hospital for pre-op. I got all checked in, IVs in, scrubbed down, gown on, paperwork signed, and then it's time. The nurse walked into the room to let me know it was time to walk to the OR. So far, everything was just like my last c-section. The anesthesiologist, Barbara, came into the room and began to put in my saddle block. Barbara messed up somehow, and I could still feel the right side of my stomach, but the left side was completely numb. The doctor and the nurses tried to talk me into letting them put me to sleep, but I refused.

If I were to be put to sleep, then that meant Matt wouldn't have been able to watch our daughter Silvia be born, and I couldn't let him miss another birth. So they continued with the c section, knowing I could feel it. Once they pulled Silvia out of my stomach, they gave me a shot of something in my IV that made the ceiling tiles move around. Silvia Mae was born 7LBS 4OZ 19 1/2 Inches.

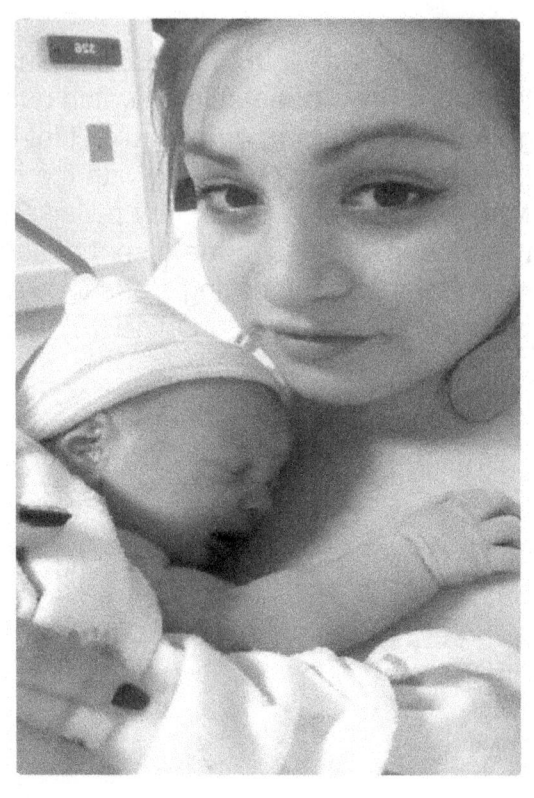

Silvia Mae
Born: May 18th, 2016
Birth Time:
Weight: 7 pounds 4 ounces
Height: 19½ inches long

Bailey Nicole Kemper

A Swift Birth

Maranda Joy Snyder

I went in at 10 am, Thursday for the foley bulb to be put in, to help me dilate. It took the doctor more than two times to get the foley bulb in because it kept falling out. I was dilated more than 2 centimeters, and the baby was low, but he got it in and sent home. By the time I got my kiddos from my moms and got home to get last minute things ready, I was contracting 7 minutes apart. Then all of a sudden they were 5 minutes and then 3. I called my hubby to come home from work, and as soon as he got back to the house, we headed to the hospital. By the time we got there, the contractions were two minutes apart. Around 10 pm, the foley bulb falls out. I'm only 4 cm baby was -1. At 9 am on Friday, they recheck me, and I'm 6 cm, and the doctor broke my water. Shortly after they started Pitocin, everything picked up quickly and got intense, so I asked for the epidural. My contractions were only a minute and a half apart.

My whole body was shaking from the pain; my contractions were intense! The doctor had trouble getting the epidural put in place, but they finally did. Once they started the first dose and took the edge off, but I felt tons of pressure and pain.

They gave me a button to push to get more doses when needed. 10:40ish the doctor checks me; 9 he says, still guessing 45 min to an hour. I told the nurse I could still feel so much; she told me the epidural doesn't take away the pressure. Although with my son, I remember I didn't feel it like that. Still, the doctor leaves, to do an inversion in another room...

I had two contractions, then I had to push. My body felt like it was trying to force itself to push my baby out. Hubby pushed the call button for the nurse. Six nurses ran into the room, one of them said,

"Look at her! Her head, it's there!"

They said don't push, but I couldn't help it; my body was forcing me. The doctor gets in, and they say to get the gloves, she right here. He jokes with them, but I barely get my legs up for a contraction and with one push her head came out! I had another contraction and pushed her body out! She was here at 11:19 pm. The doctor almost wasn't there to deliver her. I had a swift and easy labor and delivery!

Although, I felt everything because the button on the epidural didn't work! The nurses commented on how great and round the baby's head was because she wasn't in the birth canal long and came out so quickly.

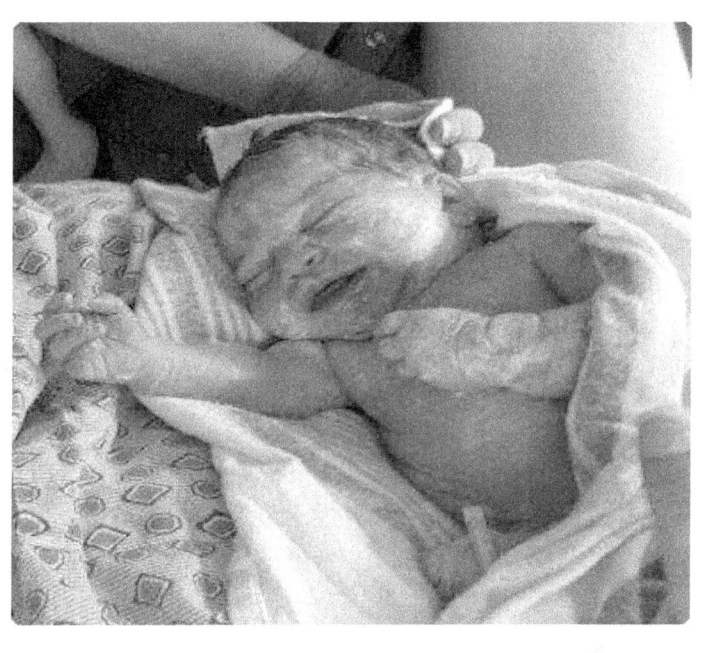

Ava Mae
Date of Birth: May 20th, 2016
Birth Time: 11:19 pm
Weight:
Height:

Maranda Joy Snyder

Maranda Joy Snyder

May 20, 2016

"Well after what seemed like forever, bulb fell out and had my bloody show. Dilated to like 4.5 but she said to her felt only 30% effaced. Contractions still 2 min apart, been having them since 1 pm. So, hopeful we progress and baby by afternoon. Till then just gave me a shot to help relax for a bit."

Maranda Joy Snyder

May 20, 2016

"Ava Mae was born today at 11:19 am."

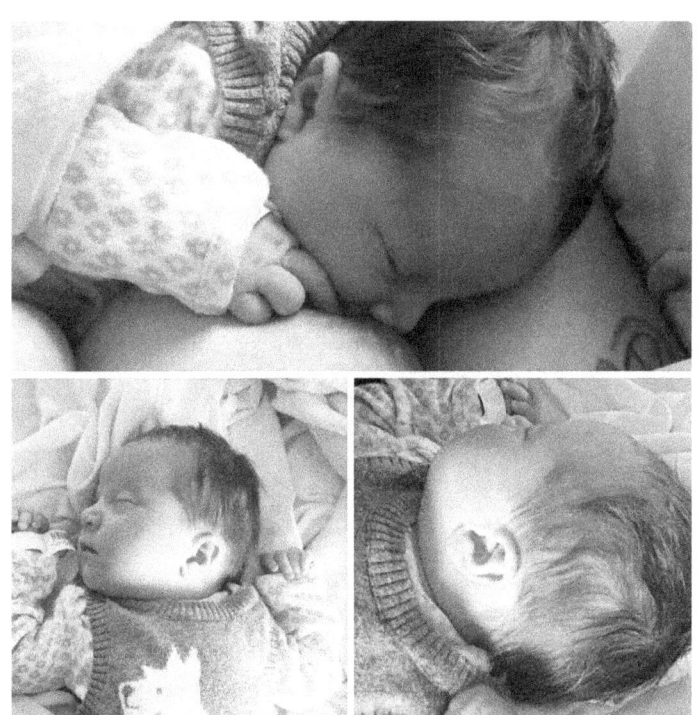

Maranda Joy Snyder

May 21, 2016

"Well her levels aren't high, they are steady medium, not
going higher or lower. So dr wants to do the light tonight
to just try and get them down"

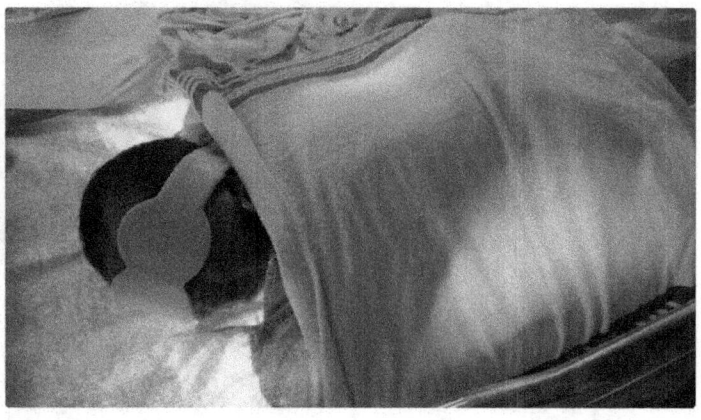

Maranda Joy Photography
www.marandajoyphotography.com

The Birth Of Eli

Linsy Porelle

My precious Eli's birth story.

After 41 weeks and 2 days, I finally went in for my induction. Which had been canceled the day before! To say I was anxious about it being canceled again was an understatement. I arrived at the labor and delivery unit at 7:30 am, to find out my best childhood friend worked there. After getting our room, settling in and getting changed, my friend came in and asked if I mind if she was my nurse, and I said,

"Absolutely Not!"

I was ecstatic and preferred it that way! There was a girl there who had been in labor for three days and wasn't progressing, and the baby was showing signs of distress, so they had to do a c section before they could start my Pitocin. At 10:27, they finally got my drip started. I was on it until around 12:30 when the OBGYN on call came in to break my waters. He wanted to know if I intended to get an epidural because if I wanted one, he would prefer they call anesthesiology before breaking my water. The doctor was afraid I may end up not getting it if it wasn't timed correctly. So the nurse called and found out the doctor was in-between surgeries, so he could do the epidural then. So, the doctor proceeded to break my waters. I was at three cms still and 80%.

Right after the doctor left the anesthesiologist, showed up. I was a bit hesitant to get the epidural right away, but because they were so busy, I thought I'd regret it if I didn't get it then. I went ahead with it, and am I ever glad I did? At 2:30 pm, the nurse and intern did another check to see if I'd progressed. In 2 hours I'd gone from 3cms to 4 and from 80% to 90%. Not very much progress, but I thought it was better than nothing. Still a bit depressing though, as I felt the epidural must have slowed things down. Around 4, I started to get excruciatingly uncomfortable. I asked my friend if the epidural was wearing off, she said that it shouldn't be. I was in so much pain, that with every contraction, I was crying. She went and got the intern and the nurse, she was working with that day. They checked my cervix, and I was fully dilated. They went out to let the OB know I was getting ready and wouldn't be too long. Around this point, it was 4:20, and they decided I should do a practice push, to see if they could get an idea of how quickly he was going to come. I did one set of practice pushes, and the nurse went to get the doctor.

The doctor came in, and he was THE BEST PUSHING COACH EVER! He was extraordinarily courteous and calm. My complete focus was on him, not that he coached me for long! After two contractions and two more sets of pushes, my beautiful boy was born at 4:30 pm on May 21st, 2016. I wouldn't change a thing about it.

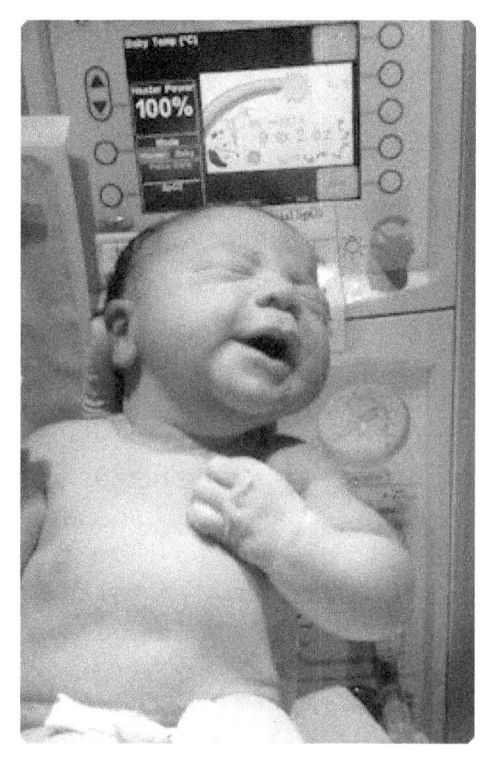

Eli Paul Cooke-Porelle
Birth Date: May 21st, 2016
Time: 4:30 pm
Weight: 9lbs 2ounces
Height: 21¼ inches

Linsy Porelle

Ten Days Overdue

Casey Lowe

My original due date was May 14th. Still, the baby was stubborn and wasn't wanting to come out on her own. So on May 24, 2016, my husband and I went to the hospital to be induced. We arrived at the hospital at 8:40 pm, and I was started on Cytotec to begin the process. Two hours later, at 10:40 pm, my daughter's heart rate started dipping after each contraction. The nurses wanted to go ahead and break my water, to hopefully help with this issue. At 11:20 pm, my doctor came in and broke my water for me. My water had meconium in it! This meant the baby had pooped in utero, and we would need additional staff on hand for the delivery, in case she needed to go to the NICU. After breaking my water, my daughter's heartbeat didn't dip as much as it had been previously. We started Pitocin at 3:45 am because my cervix hadn't dilated as much as they wanted it to. At 6 am I was finally dilated to a 6, that's when I got my epidural. Around 8 am, my husband went downstairs to the hospital cafeteria to get himself some breakfast since the process was moving so slowly. It had only been about five minutes after my husband left, my doctor came into the room to check me, and said that I had fully dilated!

I called my husband back upstairs, and at 8:40 am, I started pushing. Finally, at 11:34 am, our daughter was born!

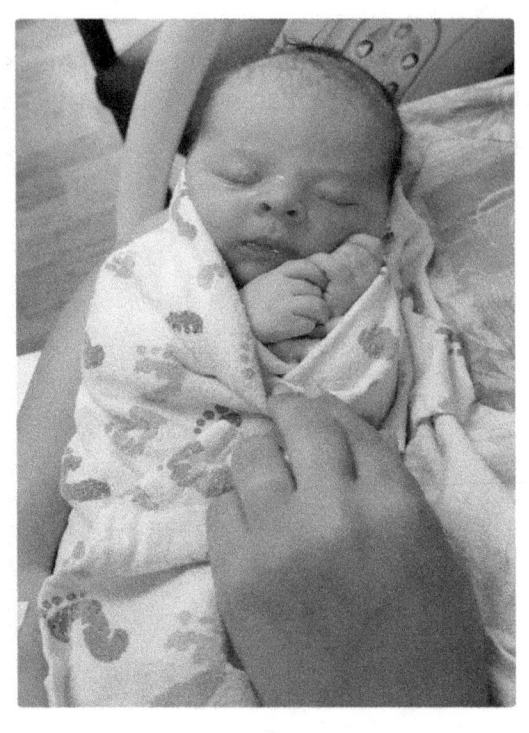

Cecilia Rose Kathleen
Date of Birth: May 25th, 2016
Time: 11:34 am
Weight: 6 pounds 10 ounces
Height: 19¾ inches long

Casey Lowe

Casey Lowe
Photographer
Studio Byrd Lowe
www.byrdlowe.com

Successful VBAC

Dana Schnyder

My contractions started at 5 pm on the 25th, and I was 40w+4d. I only had about five contractions before I went to bed that night. I woke up nearly every hour with a stronger contraction, but I never bothered to time any of them, as I thought I should sleep. In the morning, they were 8-13 mins apart, lasting 40-60 seconds. Still, they started to slow, so I walked and drank my raspberry leaf tea. By 9 pm on the 26th, I had been in active labor for 2 hours. My midwife met us at the hospital and I had my first cervical check ever...! I was 4 cm, so they admitted me into the hospital. 12 am the next morning, my contractions were one on top of the other. It was three in a row like that, then a 5-minute break in between each one. It was super weird, so my midwife went on a break. All of a sudden, I felt the need to push, and no one could find my midwife! After a bit, they found her and she re-checked my cervix, I was 9cm at 12:45 am. She asked if I would like my water broke, but I wasn't sure. I knew I needed to push, so I consented to have my waters being broken. It felt great to have the choice in my own hands! My waters were broken, at 12:49 am, and I started pushing right away. Pushed for seven minutes, and Ryker's head popped out!

The cord was around his neck, and his hands were coming out as well, I could see my sons head and face looking at me! The midwife took a moment to fix the cord and help his arms a bit, three more pushes, and he was entirely out! I only had to push for a total of 12 minutes! My VBAC was a success; I had done it! My hubby was over the moon, happy and proud of me! I wanted drugs when I was getting close but never asked. I felt like I almost couldn't do it any longer at one point, but hubby and midwife kept me going. Ryker latched great, he nursed for around 10 minutes. I labored the entire time lying on my side, while getting up in between contractions, but for me, laying on my side was just the best! I was able to get up and go pee right away after having Ryker, something I didn't get to do with my last child.

40w+5d overdue!
22 hrs of pre-labor!
7hrs of active labor!
12 mins pushing!!!
We were able to leave the hospital after only 10 hours!
No drugs!
No stitches!
Only one small tear!
I made all my own choices!
I got the birth I wanted!
The birth I needed!
I'm Not Broken!
I Can Do It!
I Did Do It!
Proud of my body!
I am a warrior!
#Successful VBAC
Thank you to all the women for your information and support in my VBAC journey!
You were all so helpful!

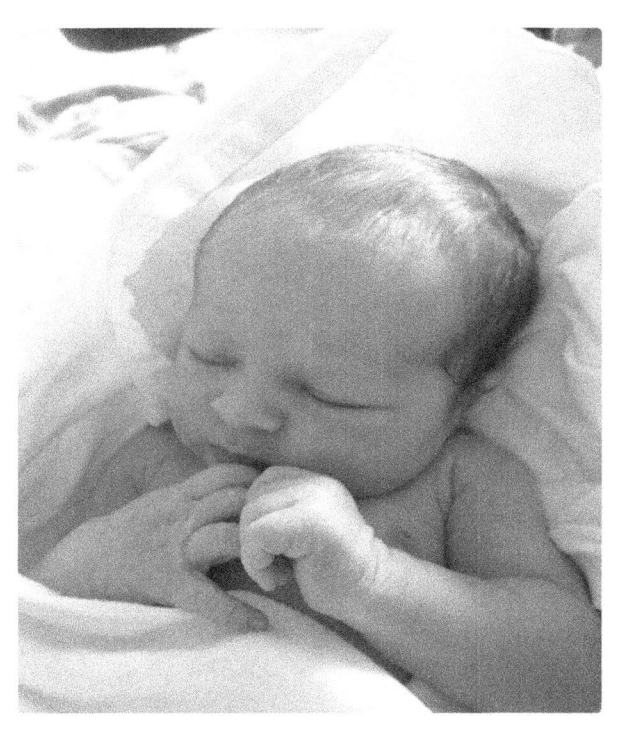

Ryker
Born at 42w + 1d
Birth Date: May 27th, 2016
Birth Time: 1:02 am
Weight: 7 pounds
Height: 20 inches long

Dana Schnyder

Repeat C-Section

Amanda Collins

My birth story is not as exciting as most. I had a repeat c-section, on the morning of Tuesday, May 31st, 2016, I arrived at the hospital for my pre-op workup. I then went home until the next morning on June 1st, when I had to go back to the hospital at 5 am. for a repeat c-section. Once I was in a pre-op room, the anesthesiologist on staff tried to give me a spinal tap. It took the doctor three tries, before deciding to give me the epidural instead. He then made four more attempts at giving me the epidural, with no success. Still, luckily for me, one of the times he had tried the spinal, it had actually worked just long enough for my c-section. Afterward, nothing was working, so they had to keep giving me IV Dilaudid. The next day, June 2nd, one of the doctors took my epidural out and just gave me the IV pain medicine. The day after that, on June 3rd, they figured out that I needed a blood patch, and that evening I got it. At first, I thought I just had terrible neck and back pain. My neck and back hurt when I would try to stand, so that's what I told the nurses. While I was laying on the recovery bed, I began to think...

'Huh?! The pain gets better when I'm laying down. I bet it's a headache at the base of my skull.'

I've never had a headache there before! I told my doctor I thought it was a headache. We decided to go ahead and do a blood patch, instead of waiting to talk to the anesthesiologist about it. I also felt some relief when the epidural was taken out. For the next 12 hours, I had to lay flat on my back, I couldn't move! My husband had to keep getting our son and handing him to me so I could even breastfeed him. It was definitely a much more complicated, and harder recovery than with my 1st c-section. Even with him having to be transferred to Texas Children's Hospital, which is about 30 minutes away, I delivered him 12 hours after, due to a heart defect. I was so determined to get out of the hospital. I wanted to see my newborn, who I only got to see for about 10 minutes before he had to be transferred to the Children's Hospital, so I pushed through the pain. I was so lonely in the hospital when I delivered my first son. My husband and my dad went with our first son to the Children's hospital, my mom stayed with me. I think the longing to be with my child is what made it much easier to recover the first time around. The staff at both hospitals were terrific! My own birth experiences are the most significant reasons I decided to become a nurse. We were treated so well in both hospitals, I wanted to do the same for other soon to be mothers and their babies.

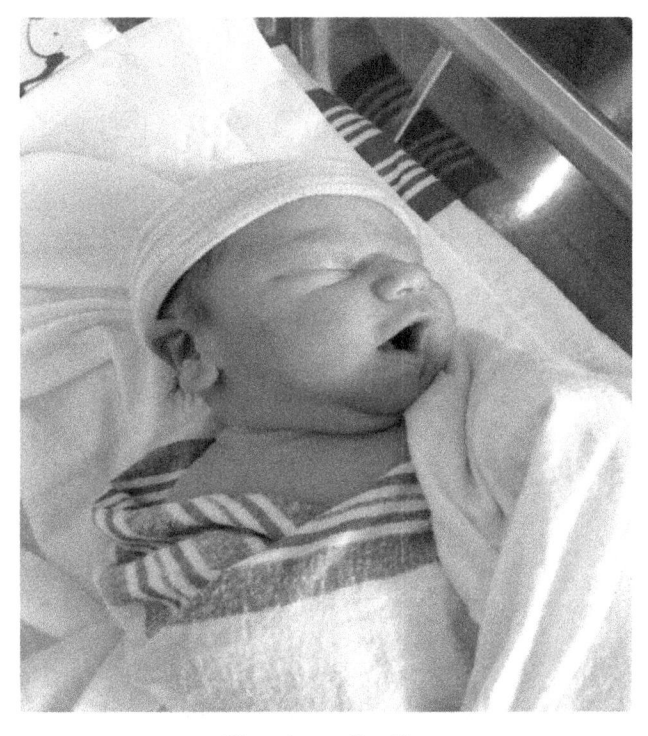

Declan Collins
Date of Birth: June 1st, 2016
Time: 8:01 am
Weight: 9 pounds 1 ounce
Height: 20 inches long

Amanda Collins

Amanda Collins

June 1, 2016

"Declan Collins born at 8:01 am 6-1-16. 9lbs 1oz 20inches long. Now we have to decide a middle name!"

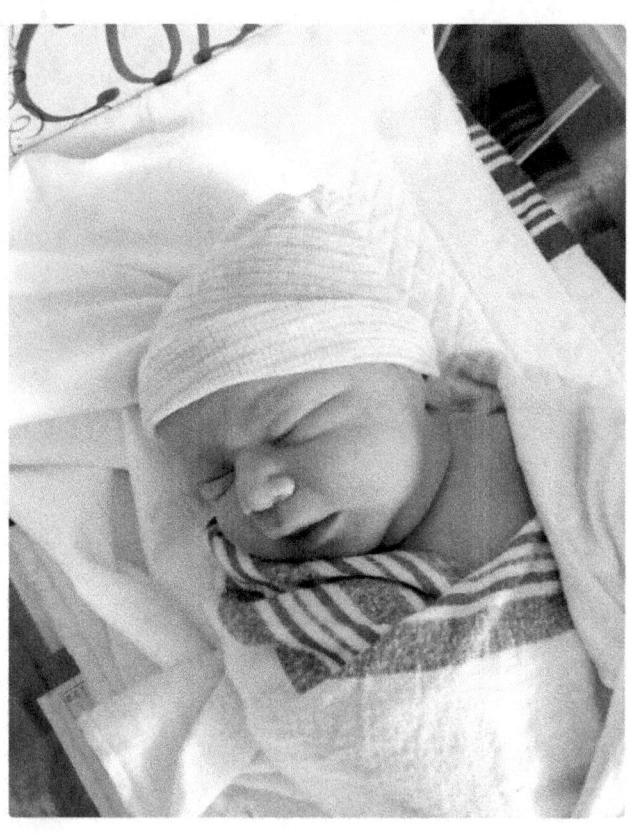

Epidural, Please!

Ashley Smith

OK, birth storytime before...

On Monday, I got checked and I was only 2cm, so my midwife stripped my membranes. Tuesday, I was a little crampy, but that's normal after I have a cervical check. On Tuesday night, we went to our friend's son's soccer game, I did a lot of walking around, and 2 hours later, I started feeling some sharp pain in my back. I went home and got everything ready for Wednesday morning. I went to bed at 1 am, and woke up at 3 am having uncomfortable contractions. I didn't sleep that much. My fiance dropped me off at the hospital at 7:30 that morning, went and dropped our son off with my family, and then he went to work. I didn't see the point of him hanging around, being grumpy and anxious, ruining my positive vibes. So I get there to be induced, and they hook me up to the monitors, to see that I'm having contractions every 3 minutes, I'm 3cm dilated and 70% effaced. We decided to give it till 12 to see if I would progress or if I'd needed the Cervidil. Contractions were uncomfortable, so I was continually walking, bouncing on a ball, and joking around with my fantastic nurse! My midwife checked me around

12:30, and I'm 4cm and still contracting, so we decided to have her break my water. She told me the contractions would get more intense.

Well, my lord, she wasn't kidding! By 1:30, I was in so much pain and begging for the epidural. I was yelling and asking someone to help me! It was embarrassing! Had the nurse call my fiance and he got there in 10 minutes. The epidural guy took forever to get to me. Then he blocks my fiance in accidentally, so he moves the table to get in front of me, to help hold me steady through the contractions. Well, since my fiance touched the table, it's now considered contaminated, and I had to wait while he went and got all-new supplies! The contractions were so severe that my body was already trying to push Macsen out. They kept telling me not to push, but I couldn't help it, with every push a ton of blood would come out of me. It was scary, but by 2:30, the epidural was in and working. I went from 4 to 7cm in an hour. I was able to relax for an hour; I could still feel the contractions, but it was more pressure than pain. My body still kept trying to push him out. The baby started showing distress, so I was given oxygen and had to keep changing positions for him, and by 3:30 I was rechecked; dilated a 10,100% effaced, and they could see and feel his hair! They told me it was time to push because the baby was ready and showing distress. Of course, my fiance had just left for the cafeteria, and ironically, the baby slowed down for a few minutes to wait for daddy to get back. I started pushing, and within 10 minutes, he was out!

I was shocked because it hardly hurt at all compared to my first; just a lot of pressure. He came out with the cord wrapped around his neck, which caused bruising. It was the longest, few minutes of my life, just waiting for him to cry! I ended up having to get two stitches and was super sore afterward, so I loaded up with pads and ice packs. Overall I was delighted that I didn't have to get induced, and my body worked its magic!

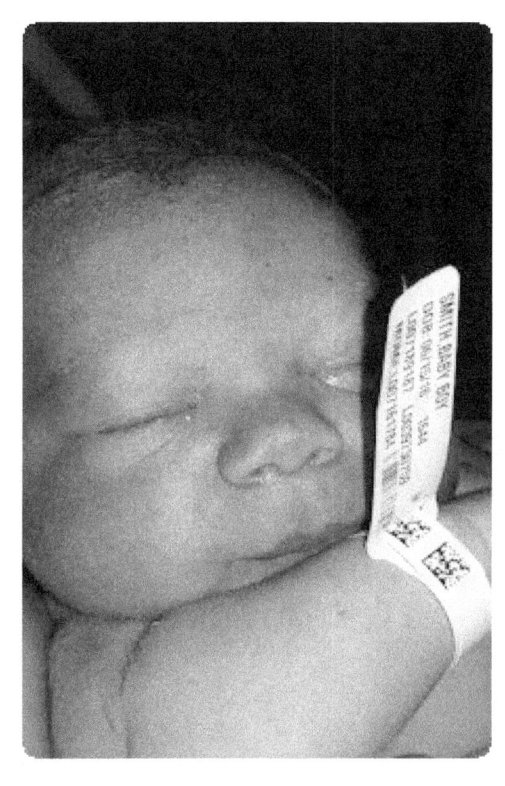

Mascen Paul
Date of Birth: June 15th, 2016
Time:
Weight: 8 pounds
Height: 21 inches

Ashley Smith

Ashley Smith

June 15, 2016

"He's here!!!

8lbs and 21 inches.

His poor face is so bruised! I'm so in love!"

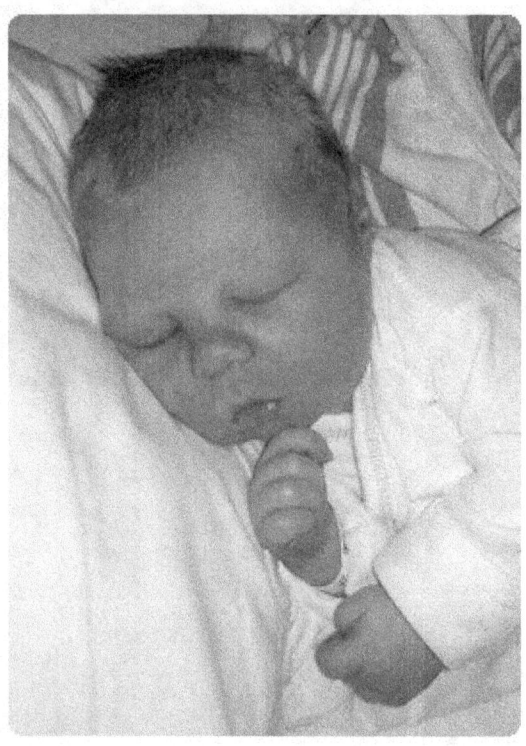

All births are "Special" and "Unique," yet not all women go into labor on their own, and some not at all, but they shouldn't feel like their bodies have failed them. Birth is "Incredible," "Beautiful" and "Powerful," no matter the circumstances.

-Real Mom's Real Birth Stories

Author Bio

Ashley Franklin is a thirty-one-year-old mother of seven. Though she has no formal education due to extenuating circumstances surrounding her childhood, later in her mid-twenties, she would receive a diagnosis of autism spectrum disorder shortly after her son. Ashley has since prevailed. Coming into her own through the rediscovery for a love of writing, she once had as a child. She is only rediscovering this passion at the age of thirty. Ashley has since gone on to self-publish an anthology of twenty-two different women's birth stories. She also has a short story featured in a children's horror anthology "Mother Ghost's Grim," as well as art in the book. She is now working on her next project while she and her husband work on illustrations for the three children's books she and her husband wrote together. Though her muse is ever-changing, writing horror is her passion.